To

From

Date

REBUILDING YOUR LIFE

Lessons From The Life And Mission of Nehemiah

A 52-Day Devotional

THE CORNERSTONE PUBLISHING

JOSEPH OLOWE

REBUILDING YOUR LIFE

Lessons from the Life and Mission of Nehemiah

Paperback ISBN: 978-1-944652-64-7

eBook ISBN: 978-1-944652-71-5

Published By:
Cornerstone Publishing
A division of Cornerstone Creativity Group LLC
Info@thecornerstonepublishers.com
www.thecornerstonepublishers.com

For booking to speak at your next event or to order bulk copies of this book please use information below:

P. O Box 10499
El Paso, TX 79995
1-800-561-9170 or +1 915-478-8807
www.drjosepholowe.com | info@drjosepholowe.com

DEDICATION

This book is dedicated to my prophet, father and revered mentor in the Lord **Bishop David Oyedepo**, whom I have never met personally but has impacted my life in many ways beyond words. I will forever be grateful for your leadership in the body of Christ and for being a perfect example for us to emulate.

ACKNOWLEDGMENTS

I will like to appreciate my savior Jesus Christ from whom all blessings flow. My sincere gratitude to my wife and partner in ministry, Omolade for her relentless pursuit of excellence for our family first and ministry.

To my children Olamide, Simi and Dare who have given me an opportunity to practice what I am preaching.

To my ministry team, first to my able editor who I consider as a gift from heaven to me, Pastor Joseph Ola and to Daniel Emonido who I refer to as mighty Danny, for all the divine graphics; many thanks.

To Pastor Gbenga Showunmi and his professional team at Cornerstone Publishing, thank you for making this dream come true.

To a good friend of mine, Pastor David Olayemi — the first man apart from my family, who sincerely believed in my writing gift and encouraged me to pursue my dream — may the God of heaven never forget your labor of love

CONTENTS

INTRODUCTION

The most common thing in life is CHANGE. The weather changes. Leadership changes. Policies change. And we — yes — we also change! Our lives do change as a result of decisions and indecisions. Some changes are trivial; others are drastic.

To cause a life-changing transformation in a child, spouse, family, job situation or even a nation involves a drastic but God-focused intervention. This was what Nehemiah did to restore the glory of God back to Jerusalem, and anyone looking for such a change can engage like Nehemiah did. Therefore, this devotional is about raising a generation of restorers like Nehemiah.

As you sincerely and holistically look at your life, community or church, you are likely to find areas that bear a close resemblance to the broken walls of Jerusalem – areas that are either not fully reflecting the promises and expectations of God for His children, or that have become outright sources of concern and reproach because they are completely broken down or in total disarray. This is why the Holy Spirit has caused this book to be written at this moment.

Like the wall of Jerusalem, your life is very important to God. And it doesn't matter how much damage that has been done to it or how long the damage has taken, it can be rebuilt and made even more glorious. All that is needed is a firm belief in the expertise of God, the Master-builder, the willingness to cooperate with Him and the commitment to the process of rebuilding, which is the central focus of this book.

More cheeringly, as you will find in the practical application of the exploit of Nehemiah contained in this book, there is no aspect of your life that cannot be built or rebuilt with the wisdom, power and guidance of the Holy Spirit. In other words, no area of your life should be in doldrums. Every part of it matters to God and He wants you to prosper, flourish and excel in each of the components (3 John 2). So, whether it is your spiritual, physical, financial, marital, emotional or professional life that you want to build or rebuild, God is reaching out to you through this book with a message of hope and that it will receive and respond to His quickening intervention. He has done it before (recall the story of the dry bones in Ezekiel 37) and He's willing and able to do it again – as long as you can cooperate with Him by following the principles outlined in this volume.

HOW TO USE THIS BOOK

This book has been prepared to be read on a day-to-day basis, over a period of 52 days. Prayerfully read through the message and Bible references for each day and meditate on them. Welcome to the journey of rebuilding your life!

Happy rebuilding!

Day 1

THE MONTH OF CHISLEU

"The words of Nehemiah the son of Hachaliah. And it came to pass in the month Chisleu, in the twentieth year, as I was in Shushan the palace." (Nehemiah 1:1)

Nehemiah had been in exile for, at least, twenty years, as revealed in the first verse and chapter of his book. And it is remarkable that it was at this point in his life that he began the historic rebuilding process, for which he is most remembered. What this means for you is that it does not matter how long your situation has been in disarray or how long you seem to have delayed to act - today prophetically marks the beginning of your month of Chisleu.

The most striking thing about this period in Jerusalem was its seeming lifelessness and hopelessness. Indeed, the state of affairs in Jerusalem can be likened to the initial state of the universe in Genesis—without form and void, and with darkness all over the place. Simply put, there was no existence of LIFE. You may consider this to be an adequate description of your situation but, believe me, today marks the dawning of a new day for you.

Start With Questions

> *"That Hanani, one of my brethren, came, he and certain men of Judah; and I asked them concerning the Jews that had escaped, which were left of the captivity, and concerning Jerusalem. And they said unto me, The remnant that are left of the captivity there in the province are in great affliction and reproach: the wall of Jerusalem also is broken down, and the gates thereof are burned with fire." (Nehemiah 1:2-3).*

Transformation and restoration are preceded by asking soul-searching questions that set the questioner on a course of collision with destiny. It is time to pick up your pen and start writing in your journal provided with this devotional. Ask yourself some honest and soul-searching questions about the situation you are currently facing. Nehemiah began from there. He asked Hanani concerning the Jews that had escaped, which were left of the captivity and concerning Jerusalem. Hanani replied that the remnant that were left of the captivity were in great affliction and reproach, and that the wall of Jerusalem was broken down and the gates burned.

That is where transformation begins—taking a complete inventory of your life and spotting areas of unproductivity or of complete darkness. For a greater outcome in life, you need to develop an accountability system which is built around asking relevant questions that will make your victory sure and evident for all to see.

THE TIME OF LIFE

That the course of transformation which Nehemiah embarked

upon began in the month of Chisleu was not a mere coincidence. Evidence from the Scripture shows that there is something unique about that month, which is worth noting. Genesis 18:9-10, for instance, reveals: *"And they said unto him, Where is Sarah thy wife? And he said, Behold, in the tent. And he said, I will certainly return unto thee according to the time of life; and, lo, Sarah thy wife shall have a son. And Sarah heard it in the tent door, which was behind him."*

In the Jewish calendar, the month of Chisleu is the ninth month and the ninth month in God's calendar is the TIME OF LIFE. It is also noteworthy that before Isaac was conceived - after many decades of barrenness - the angels of the Lord asked Abraham a question: Where is Sarah your wife? (This was the same way Nehemiah asked Hanani the question that led to the restoration he would lead); and in the following month of Chisleu (nine months after the angelic visitation) which is the 'time of life', Sarah brought forth a new life—Isaac.

In the mouth of two or three witnesses, the truth is established. This is a biblical principle for establishing the truth; therefore, we will consider another similar example from 2 Kings 4: 14-16:

> *"And he said, What then is to be done for her? And Gehazi answered, Verily she hath no child, and her husband is old. And he said, Call her. And when he had called her, she stood in the door. And he said, About this season, according to the time of life, thou shalt embrace a son. And she said, Nay, my lord, thou man of God, do not lie unto thine handmaid."*

Prophet Elisha asked concerning the Shunammite woman: "What then is to be done for her"? Here was a woman who had been very helpful to the ministry of Elisha, but she was barren. Gehazi, the servant of Elisha, answered the question, "She has no child" (that is, there's no sign of life in the house). Hence, Elisha prophesied that according to the TIME OF LIFE, she would give birth to a son, and lo, in the month of Chisleu as it were, she brought forth a baby boy.

Again, as we have seen in each of the examples above, for any restoration to take place, there's a great need to start asking some serious and thought-provoking questions. If there has been no evidence of LIFE in your life, marriage, business, job, family, finance or relationships, then you are at the right place and right time to start asking questions about your situation. I am persuaded that this is your month of Chisleu—the time of life for you is now! If you are sincere with yourself, according to the time of life (within the next nine months) your situation will change for the better.

Of course, the time of life may vary for the different situations you might be facing; but one fact remains constant: you will end up with LIFE—the God-kind of life—permeating all your endeavors. The question God is asking you today is: "Where art thou"? (Genesis 3:9). Your answer will determine what your next course of action will be.

WORDS TO PONDER ON...

"At the end it shall speak!"

> *"For the vision is yet for an appointed time, but at the end it shall speak, and not lie: though it tarry, wait for it; because it will surely come, it will not tarry." (Habakkuk 2:3).*

Beloved, your end result will not keep quiet; it will speak out loud! Your vision of building or rebuilding every area of your life will be a reality.

ASSIGNMENT

1. Write down relevant questions and answers that will aid your rebuilding process.
2. Determine where you are, based on the question God is asking you.
3. Ask in prayer and maybe, with fasting, the clear pathway to pursue.

Day 2

I AM NEHEMIAH

"And it came to pass, when I heard these words, that I sat down and wept, and mourned certain days, and fasted, and prayed before the God of heaven." (Nehemiah 1:4)

Who was Nehemiah? Nehemiah means "Yahweh Comforts", the long version of the name "Nahum" which also means "Comforter". It is only God that can comfort and bring a complete restoration. Jesus told us when He was leaving that He would send us a comforter that would remind us all things and would also help in our daily battles (John 14:26). So, the question is, Where are the Nehemiahs of this generation? Are you a Nehemiah for your family?

"But Jesus beheld them, and said unto them, With men this is impossible; but with God all things are possible." (Matthew 19:26)

Nehemiah was a cupbearer for the king in a strange land and in a kingdom that did not believe in the God of the Jews. All odds were stacked against him to make any major progress. Similarly, all odds may be against you today in your quest for a new beginning, but remember that with God, all things are possible.

Let us consider the assignment that Nehemiah was up against. His assignment comprised four major segments: the task, the target, the tool and the time—none of which was in any way favorable.

THE TASK

What Was The Task?

The task for Nehemiah was to rebuild the wall of Jerusalem and to improve the quality of life for the remnant left behind. At a first look, this job seems beyond his capability. He thus could have come up with various plausible reasons why the task was an impossible one. He was in a strange land, serving a strange king; there was no financial support in sight; and he did not know if he would be welcomed by his people.

In a striking parallel, think about it - what are you up against today? Like Nehemiah, there might be one million reasons why the wall you are trying to rebuild may seem impossible, but never lose sight of the fact that what God did for one He can do for another. You are up to the task. Like Caleb and Joshua, rise up at once and take over that mountain! *"And Caleb stilled the people before Moses, and said, Let us go up at once, and possess it; for we are well able to overcome it." (Numbers 13:30).*

THE TARGET

What Was The Target?

There were two targets that Nehemiah had to deal with and both targets were highly unpredictable and could cost him his life. The first was King Artaxerxes—for whom he was a cupbearer. Being the king's cupbearer, Nehemiah was not expected to be sad for any reason. His position with the king was so sensitive that if the king suspected any change in his disposition, it was an automatic prison sentence or death. The second target were the Jews that he had not seen for more than twenty years. He didn't know if he would be welcomed back in Jerusalem. Despite these two great challenges, Nehemiah decided to proceed with his plan to rebuild the wall and he found favor on both sides.

What challenges are you facing today? What are the targets that seem insurmountable to accomplish your set goals? Like Nehemiah, be prepared to risk it all, because greater is He that is in you than that situation you are facing. Saul and his army saw Goliath as a target insurmountable, but David saw him as a target that was too big to miss. Like David, rise up at once and bring down that target now. *"And David put his hand in his bag, and took thence a stone, and slang it, and smote the Philistine in his forehead, that the stone sunk into his forehead; and he fell upon his face to the earth." (1 Samuel 17:49).*

THE TOOL

What Tool Did Nehemiah Employ?

Viewed realistically, the tools needed by a man in slavery to successfully execute an assignment like that of Nehemiah are beyond his reach. The money, the manpower, the negotiations, the paperwork and other essential requirements, as evident in Nehemiah's narrative, would have constituted a major barrier to the success of such a venture. And so it appeared in the case of Nehemiah. It seemed impossible for him to get the necessary tools to accomplish the task, but quite significantly, he found FAVOR with the king and other authorities, as well as his people — except for a few nefarious individuals that we will later discuss.

One tool however that our verse for today pointed out is the twin pillars of fasting and prayer. The Bible is replete with powerful verses that deal with this very subject. We will touch on fasting here and Nehemiah's prayer in the next chapter.

The most fascinating question about fasting is contained in Isaiah 58:5, *"Is it such a fast that I have chosen?"* In other words, there is a type of fast or the way to fast that will effect the greatest change anticipated in a given situation. The answers are expressly given in the verses that follow. A fasting day is not a day for a man or woman to show off his or her humility by putting on a sanctimonious long face or parading around solemnly in black— this is not the type of fast that will bring results. Rather, God demands that our fasting days should be days to break the chain of injustice, to get rid of exploitation in the workplace, to free the oppressed, to cancel debts.

Essentially, the kind of fast that delights God and gets results is such that involves charitable deeds — sharing your food with the hungry, providing for the homeless, covering the naked and being there for your own family. Here is the entire passage in Isaiah:

> *"Is it such a fast that I have chosen? a day for a man to afflict his soul? is it to bow down his head as a bulrush, and to spread sackcloth and ashes under him? wilt thou call this a fast, and an acceptable day to the Lord? Is not this the fast that I have chosen? to loose the bands of wickedness, to undo the heavy burdens, and to let the oppressed go free, and that ye break every yoke? Is it not to deal thy bread to the hungry, and that thou bring the poor that are cast out to thy house? when thou seest the naked, that thou cover him; and that thou hide not thyself from thine own flesh?" (Isaiah 58:5-7)*

As we faithfully follow this divine blueprint, our fasts will command outstanding results. Some of these results are outlined in the succeeding verses paraphrased thus: then shall your light break forth as the morning (CLARITY OF VISION), your health shall spring forth speedily (DIVINE STRENGTH), your righteousness shall go before you (RIGHT STANDING WITH GOD), the glory of God shall be thy reward (YOU BECOME A STANDARD), you will call and the Lord will answer (COMMANDING RESULTS), and you shall cry and the Lord will be your standing up and recovery (THE GREAT I AM).

God requires from us a few more things in the day of fasting. He wants us to get rid of: unfair practices, blaming victims, and gossiping about other people's sin. Instead, we must be generous with the hungry and start giving ourselves to the down-and-out. When all these acts come together, then you are about to start the rebuilding process like Nehemiah. The Bible further reveals the rewards of such a fast: your light will rise from obscurity (TIME OF FAVOR) and your darkness as a noonday (DIVINE DISCOVERIES); the Lord will guide you continually (DIVINE GUIDANCE), satisfy your soul in drought (DIVINE PROVISION), make fat your bone (FATNESS OF SPIRIT), and you shall be a watered garden and spring of water whose water fails not (FRUIT-BEARING LIFESTYLE).

> *"Then shall thy light break forth as the morning, and thine health shall spring forth speedily: and thy righteousness shall go before thee; the glory of the Lord shall be thy rearward. Then shalt thou call, and the Lord shall answer; thou shalt cry, and he shall say, Here I am. If thou take away from the midst of thee the yoke, the putting forth of the finger, and speaking vanity; And if thou draw out thy soul to the hungry, and satisfy the afflicted soul; then shall thy light rise in obscurity, and thy darkness be as the noonday: And the Lord shall*

guide thee continually, and satisfy thy soul in drought, and make fat thy bones: and thou shalt be like a watered garden, and like a spring of water, whose waters fail not. And they that shall be of thee shall build the old waste places: thou shalt raise up the foundations of many generations; and thou shalt be called, The repairer of the breach, The restorer of paths to dwell in" (Isaiah 58:8-12).

It is of particular interest that the Scripture assures that if you can diligently go through the process of rebuilding all that needs to be rebuilt in your life, generations to come after you will continue to benefit from your determination to change the course of your destiny. It says, "They that shall be of thee shall build the old waste places and raise up the foundations of many generations." For your determination to engage and effect a lasting change, your name shall be called THE REPAIRER OF THE BREACH and THE RESTORER OF THE PATHS TO DWELL IN.

Jesus also explicitly instructed us on the subject of fasting. He made it clear that fasting is not an optional vocation for the believer. (He did not say "Moreover IF ye fast…", He said "Moreover WHEN ye fast…"). He Himself fasted for forty days and returned in the power of the Spirit for greater exploits to become the greatest rebuilder this world has ever known. He reiterated the message of Isaiah 58 as he taught against hypocritical fasting.

"Moreover when ye fast, be not, as the hypocrites, of a sad countenance: for they disfigure their faces, that they may appear unto men to fast. Verily I say unto you, They have their reward. But thou, when thou fastest, anoint thine head, and wash thy face; That thou appear not unto men to fast, but unto thy Father which is in secret: and thy Father, which seeth in secret, shall reward thee openly" (Matthew 6:16-18).

"And Jesus being full of the Holy Ghost returned from Jordan, and was led by the Spirit into the wilderness, being forty days tempted of

the devil. And in those days he did eat nothing: and when they were ended, he afterward hungered. And Jesus returned in the power of the Spirit into Galilee: and there went out a fame of him through all the region round about." (Luke 4:1-2, 14).

Like Jesus, Nehemiah modeled these qualities and it was clear that he became the rebuilder of the wall with no breach left in. His story can challenge us to summon up the courage for the journey of a lifetime.

What are your excuses today? What is that one thing you are waiting for? Friend, the cattle upon a thousand hills belongs to God! (Psalm 50:10). The manpower you need is already being notified—remember, the heart of the king is in His hands (Proverbs 21:1). You have all you need to take up the mountain! Inside of you is JESUS, the hope of glory. Come on, let's get going!

Peter and John did not have gold and silver for the man at the beautiful gate (Acts 3:6), but that did not stop them from moving the mountain in the cripple's life. Today, heaven has endowed you with all the fullness of God. You have what it takes. You have the tools you need!

THE TIME

What Time Was It?

There is never a convenient time for progress to be made. Nehemiah was constrained on time; he would need the permission of the king and make other arrangements for his daily duties not to be affected. Perhaps he also had to make an arrangement with his family, and on and on it goes. In short, the timing is never right to rise and rebuild any wall that has broken down in our lives. But against all odds and timing constraints, Nehemiah made a request to the king and he was able to go.

What are your excuses about time? Are you worried about how long it will take? Remember, there is time and season for everything (Ecclesiastes 3:1). Your time on earth is limited, even if you spend one hundred and twenty years. But the constraint of time shouldn't limit you because your God changes times and seasons so as to accommodate your uplifting. So, get your marching order and move on!

Here's what David said, God will rise on your behalf and have mercy because you dwell in Zion and your set TIME of favor has come. It is not 'going to come'; it is here already!

> *"Thou shalt arise, and have mercy upon Zion: for the time to favour her, yea, the set time, is come." (Psalms 102:13).*

The task is not going to be easy, but accept it anyway; the target(s) might be ever moving, but still aim and shoot; the tool(s) might not be with you, but remember Jehovah Jireh; and lastly, it might not seem like the right time, but start with some baby steps, because it is going to be precepts upon precepts and line upon line, but you must get to your promised land. "For precept must be upon precept, precept upon precept; line upon line, line upon line; here a little, and there a little." (Isaiah 28:10).

WORDS TO PONDER ON...

"God is looking for Nehemiahs"

> *"And I sought for a man among them, that should make up the hedge, and stand in the gap before me for the land, that I should not destroy it: but I found none." (Ezekiel 22:30).*

Are you ready to be the next Nehemiah? God is looking for any man or woman who will work with Him to repair the breach.

ASSIGNMENT

1. Define your task(s)
2. Define your target(s)
3. Define your tool(s)
4. Define your timeline(s)

Day 3

PRAYER OF NEHEMIAH

"And said, I beseech thee, O Lord God of heaven, the great and terrible God, that keepeth covenant and mercy for them that love him and observe his commandments:" (Nehemiah 1:5)

Any meaningful and lasting transformation or restoration will begin in the place of prayer, for it is "not by might, nor by power, but by my spirit, saith the Lord of hosts." (Zechariah 4:6). It took Jesus forty days of prayer and fasting to be ready for a three-and a-half-year ministry. You and I have been here for some time and will be here for much longer than thirty-three-and-a-half years! We must be willing to engage in prayer to rebuild and fulfill our destiny. Nehemiah prayed for the situation of things in Jerusalem as was described to him; let us look at the content of his prayer and learn.

NEHEMIAH'S PRAYER POINTS

PRAYER 1

> *"And said, I beseech thee, O Lord God of heaven, the great and terrible God, that keepeth covenant and mercy for them that love him and observe his commandments:" (Nehemiah 1:5)*

In your prayer, seek to get God's attention. Nehemiah said "I beseech thee…" To beseech is to implore urgently. If your prayer does not have any sense of urgency, it will not move you, let alone move God. God is great and awesome—greater than any problem you will ever have—and He keeps covenant and mercy for them that love Him and observe His commandments. Are you born again? If you are not, God is not obligated to keep up with you.

PRAYER 2

> *"Let thine ear now be attentive, and thine eyes open, that thou mayest hear the prayer of thy servant, which I pray before thee now, day and night, for the children of Israel thy servants, and confess the sins of the children of Israel, which we have sinned against thee: both I and my father's house have sinned. We have dealt very corruptly against thee, and have not kept the commandments, nor the statutes, nor the judgments, which thou commandedst thy servant Moses." (Nehemiah 1:6-7)*

Nehemiah is taking his rightful place in prayer. In Isaiah 45:11, we are instructed to command Him (GOD). As such, Nehemiah is telling God to be attentive, to open His eyes that He may hear his prayer, which he's praying and will be praying day and night. In approaching God in prayers, do not go as a beggar; go as one with authority. Furthermore, Nehemiah repented of his sins and for the people.

"Thus saith the Lord, the Holy One of Israel, and his Maker, Ask me of things to come concerning my sons, and concerning the work of my hands command ye me." (Isaiah 45:11)

PRAYER 3

"Remember, I beseech thee, the word that thou commandedst thy servant Moses, saying, If ye transgress, I will scatter you abroad among the nations: But if ye turn unto me, and keep my commandments, and do them; though there were of you cast out unto the uttermost part of the heaven, yet will I gather them from thence, and will bring them unto the place that I have chosen to set my name there." (Nehemiah 1:8-9)

Nehemiah reminded God His own very words. When someone reminds you of what you had said earlier, it is very likely that you will pause and reconsider the request of the person. In prayer, praying the word of God guarantees answers to one's request. 1 John 5:14 tells us that if we ask Him anything according to His will—and His will is His word—He hears us. "And this is the confidence that we have in him, that, if we ask anything according to his will, he heareth us." (1 John 5:14)

PRAYER 4

"Now these are thy servants and thy people, whom thou hast redeemed by thy great power, and by thy strong hand." (Nehemiah 1:10).

Nehemiah reaffirmed his position as a child of God; he placed a demand on his redemptive rights, thus reminding God the cost of his sonship. The blood of Jesus is the most precious blood that will ever be sacrificed, and it has fully paid for everything you will ever need in your life. We are redeemed by the blood without blemish, and that should mean something. *"Forasmuch as ye know that ye were not redeemed with corruptible things, as silver and gold, from your vain conversation received by tradition from your fathers; But with the precious blood of Christ, as of a lamb without blemish and without spot." (1 Peter 1:18-19)*

PRAYER 5

> *"O Lord, I beseech thee, let now thine ear be attentive to the prayer of thy servant, and to the prayer of thy servants, who desire to fear thy name: and prosper, I pray thee, thy servant this day, and grant him mercy in the sight of this man. For I was the king's cupbearer." (Nehemiah 1:11)*

Nehemiah was very specific in his request; he was not all over the place. He asked God to grant him mercy and favor in the sight of the king. In prayer, we must be specific in our requests. An apt case study is the blind man that asked Jesus for help. When he was brought to Jesus, He asked him a question, "What do you want me to do for you?" He answered and said "I want to receive my sight." (Mark 10:51). Be specific in your prayer and your answer will come knocking.

WORDS TO PONDER ON...

"Before you call…"

> *"And it shall come to pass, that before they call, I will answer; and while they are yet speaking, I will hear." (Isaiah 65:24)*

This is a special promise from God. He says that before you pray, He will answer and while you are yet speaking He will hear. With this promise in view, go ahead and make that request.

ASSIGNMENT

1. Understand your right standing with God.
2. List out your prayer points.
3. Be specific in your request.
4. Engage with His promises in the word.

Day 4

PLANNING FOR REBUILDING

"And it came to pass in the month Nisan, in the twentieth year of Artaxerxes the king, that wine was before him: and I took up the wine, and gave it unto the king. Now I had not been beforetime sad in his presence." (Nehemiah 2:1)

FROM CHISLEU TO NISAN

As we earlier noted, Chisleu is the ninth month of the Jewish calendar; and it was the month in which Nehemiah got the report of the situation of things in Jerusalem. But he did not make any move until the month of Nisan. The month of Nisan is a spring month, usually in March or April. 'Nisan' means happiness, redemption and salvation—it is the Passover month. What was Nehemiah doing between Chisleu and Nisan? He was very patiently processing the situation. It takes time and adequate planning for a successful rebuilding project. In other words, rebuilding is a systematic process, involving a number of steps and stages.

STAGE 1

You Cannot Build At A Distance

It is extremely difficult to rebuild from a distance. Nehemiah could have gathered all the necessary equipment and made all the arrangements and then instruct Hanani to start the work of rebuilding. That would have been the easiest thing to do, but not Nehemiah. You cannot effect any lasting change from a distance and by delegation. You must be present and take the bull by the horn. Remember, you are Nehemiah.

Time Estimations

As discussed earlier, the need for establishing timelines is very important and can only be done by you.

Connecting The Dots From Point A to B

Nobody can connect the dots for you. Nehemiah went to the king and appealed to his kinsmen for the rebuilding to be successful. Like Nehemiah, you are also going to need the King (GOD) and your kinsmen (PEOPLE) to help in the process. And guess what? You are the only connection between the two. God will walk with you and move the heart of people to help your cause in the rebuilding process.

What Do You Need to Start the Process of Rebuilding?

You might not know all that you are going to need; Nehemiah did not know either. He began with the most important task—he engaged the king. You too can start today by engaging the King of kings (GOD). No more delays!

Time to Engage

The time is now. After Nehemiah had prepared himself, he engaged in the month of Nisan. As already noted, Nisan means happiness, redemption and salvation—it is the Passover month. Prophetically speaking, now is the time to pass over the obstacles holding you back.

Communication

> *"And said unto the king, Let the king live forever: why should not my countenance be sad, when the city, the place of my fathers' sepulchres, lieth waste, and the gates thereof are consumed with fire?" (Nehemiah 2:3)*

Effective communication is one of most powerful tools you are going to need to help with the rebuilding process, either with the king or the people.

What is Your Request?

> *"Then the king said unto me, For what dost thou make request? So I prayed to the God of heaven." (Nehemiah 2:4)*

For anybody to commit to helping you, you must have an idea of what you need. It is not compulsory to have a clear detail of everything you will need but, at least, an idea so that you can communicate effectively.

Specificity

> *"And I said unto the king, If it please the king, and if thy servant have found favour in thy sight, that thou wouldest send me unto Judah, unto the city of my fathers' sepulchres, that I may build it." (Nehemiah 2:5)*

Being specific with one's request is not only a good but a must-have virtue. Whether your request is to God or people, be specific. When you are specific, help and answers will come rather quickly and steadily.

Timetable

> *"And the king said unto me, (the queen also sitting by him,) For how long shall thy journey be? and when wilt thou return? So it pleased the king to send me; and I set him a time." (Nehemiah 2:6)*

Rebuilding anything, however daunting the task may be, always has a start and an end time. It is also a sign of serious-mindedness for an individual to have a sense of timing. There's nothing wrong with readjusting your timetable, but having no idea of your timetable signifies a dead project before it even gets off ground.

The Place of Authority

> *"Moreover I said unto the king, If it please the king, let letters be given me to the governors beyond the river, that they may convey me over till I come into Judah;" (Nehemiah 2:7).*

A life without an established authority will eventually crash. The need to submit to authority not only gives a person coverage but affords such individual with leverage and latitude. Nehemiah acknowledged and respected every authority; therefore the rebuilding process became much easier. He also had the respect of whoever he encountered. Like Nehemiah, embrace your need to acknowledge and submit to God-ordained authority in your life, whether at home or civil authority. This will give you the most needed structure on which you can begin your building or rebuilding process.

The Budgeting

"And a letter unto Asaph the keeper of the king's forest, that he may give me timber to make beams for the gates of the palace which appertained to the house, and for the wall of the city, and for the house that I shall enter into. And the king granted me, according to the good hand of my God upon me." (Nehemiah 2:8)

This is where the rubber meets the road. There must be a clear budget for the process, both in terms of finance and emotions. If you are weak in this area, please ask questions and seek help from the right sources. As Nehemiah had a team behind him, likewise, recognize your team for this rebuilding effort. Understand that without a budget, you might end up creating another hole that would need repairs or rebuilding later.

The Security

"Then I came to the governors beyond the river, and gave them the king's letters. Now the king had sent captains of the army and horsemen with me." (Nehemiah 2:9)

Have you thought about your security? Rebuilding will sometimes require adequate security, especially when dealing with a delicate relationship. Nehemiah quickly realized the need for security on his journey against nefarious people, like you are most likely to encounter in your own journey. Your security is paramount because without you, any rebuilding project stops. Cheeringly, in addition to the steps you take to ensuring your security, you have a great assurance of divine security in Isaiah 54:17: *"No weapon that is formed against thee shall prosper; and every tongue that shall rise against thee in judgment thou shalt condemn. This is the heritage of the servants of the Lord, and their righteousness is of me, saith the Lord."*

WORDS TO PONDER ON...

"His thoughts are different"

> *"For my thoughts are not your thoughts, neither are your ways my ways, saith the Lord." (Isaiah 55:8)*

Adequate planning will get you in tune with God. If you fail to plan, then you have planned to fail. His thought will make your building or rebuilding efforts easy.

ASSIGNMENT

1. Develop a good communication strategy.
2. Acknowledge and submit to appropriate authority.
3. Develop a working budget.
4. Determine your security risk (if there is any).

Day 5

A THOROUGH ASSESSMENT

STAGE 2

1. Know Your Adversaries

"When Sanballat the Horonite, and Tobiah the servant, the Ammonite, heard of it, it grieved them exceedingly that there was come a man to seek the welfare of the children of Israel." (Nehemiah 2:10)

Nehemiah identified quickly who his enemies were. Knowing your adversaries helps you develop a good fighting strategy. Like Nehemiah, how quickly you can identify your enemies of progress determines how quickly you can conquer them.

2. Get Involved in the Situation

"So I came to Jerusalem, and was there three days." (Nehemiah 2:11)

Here, Nehemiah established a standard—a three-day process in his own case. It was emphasized earlier that you cannot solve your problem from a distance. Here, Nehemiah takes things further by introducing to us to the principle of involvement—taking a second look at the situation or problem up-close-and-personal. Why do you need this? Among other things, it will afford you the opportunity to come up with a good team to tackle the problem.

3. Keep Your Mouth Sealed

> *"And I arose in the night, I and some few men with me; neither told I any man what my God had put in my heart to do at Jerusalem: neither was there any beast with me, save the beast that I rode upon." (Nehemiah 2:12)*

If you cannot say anything positive, please refrain from negativity. If you are the type that talks too much, it is very possible to talk yourself out of taking the appropriate steps to start your rebuilding process. There are many naysayers out there who will agree with you that repairing or rebuilding your life is a waste of time. Nehemiah kept everything to himself until he was able to find the right team for his project. Your tongue is the greatest weapon for or against you.

4. Take a Second Look

> *"And I went out by night by the gate of the valley, even before the dragon well, and to the dung port, and viewed the walls of Jerusalem, which were broken down, and the gates thereof were consumed with fire. Then I went on to the gate of the fountain, and to the king's pool: but there was no place for the beast that was under me to pass. Then went I up in the night by the brook, and viewed the wall, and turned back, and entered by the gate of the valley, and so returned." (Nehemiah 2:13-15)*

This is what Nehemiah did for three days—having a good second look. Every problem needs a second gaze.

5. Build Up A Team

> *"And the rulers knew not whither I went, or what I did; neither had I as yet told it to the Jews, nor to the priests, nor to the nobles, nor to the rulers, nor to the rest that did the work. Then said I unto them, Ye see the distress that we are in, how Jerusalem lieth waste, and the gates thereof are burned with fire: come, and let us build up the wall of Jerusalem, that we be no more a reproach. Then I told them of the hand of my God which was good upon me; as also the king's words that he had spoken unto me. And they said, Let us rise up and build. So they strengthened their hands for this good work." (Nehemiah 2:16-18)*

It is time to build the team. You don't need to do this alone, help is available everywhere. A good communication of what you are trying to accomplish is a good place to start. After sharing this, you can quickly establish who is with you. You may need different teams for different projects but these two things will remain constant: God and people—and in that order—then, you are on your way to building a great and formidable team.

6. Set Your Expectations at the Beginning

> *"But when Sanballat the Horonite, and Tobiah the servant, the Ammonite, and Geshem the Arabian, heard it, they laughed us to scorn, and despised us, and said, What is this thing that ye do? will ye rebel against the king? Then answered I them, and said unto them, The God of heaven, he will prosper us; therefore we his servants will arise and build: but ye have no portion, nor right, nor memorial, in Jerusalem." (Nehemiah 2:19-20)*

Like Nehemiah, set your expectations at the beginning, otherwise you will find yourself on an unpleasant track, even with the best team. Enemies of progress are everywhere to derail you. *"For surely there is an end; and thine expectation shall not be cut off." (Proverbs 23:18)*

WORDS TO PONDER ON...

"Count the cost"

A thorough assessment will help you with how to develop an effective strategy to ensure that your building or rebuilding effort is not frustrated.

"For which of you, intending to build a tower, sitteth not down first, and counteth the cost, whether he have sufficient to finish it?" (Luke 14:28)

ASSIGNMENT

1. Identify your adversaries.
2. Watch your tongue.
3. Give it a second look.
4. Develop your team.
5. Set your expectations.

Day 6

FIRST THING FIRST

"Then said I unto them, Ye see the distress that we are in, how Jerusalem lieth waste, and the gates thereof are burned with fire: come, and let us build up the wall of Jerusalem, that we be no more a reproach." (Nehemiah 2:17)

Rebuilding without an appropriate foundation amounts to a wasted effort. Nehemiah was ready to start right; he said, "look at the distress we are in, how Jerusalem lies in waste and the gates thereof are burned with fire." So he made a plan to rebuild and restore the glory of Jerusalem. He had only ONE purpose of rebuilding and that was to remove REPROACH.

A life without Christ is full of reproach; and any attempt to build or rebuild it without first establishing a solid relationship with Christ is a total waste of time. It is time to do the first thing first. Nicodemus did this. He came to Jesus to strike up a conversation and to really get close to Jesus so that he too could rebuild his life with Jesus. Jesus quickly changed the subject and went to the heart of the matter with Nicodemus: "Except a man be born again, he cannot see the kingdom of God" (John 3:3).

The process of rebuilding a life that will endure to the end begins with Jesus. Ephesians 2:12-16 shows that a life without Christ is alienated from the commonwealth of Israel, a stranger from the covenants of promise, having no hope and without God.

> *"That at that time ye were without Christ, being aliens from the commonwealth of Israel, and strangers from the covenants of promise, having no hope, and without God in the world: But now in Christ Jesus ye who sometimes were far off are made nigh by the blood of Christ. For he is our peace, who hath made both one, and hath broken down the middle wall of partition between us; Having abolished in his flesh the enmity, even the law of commandments contained in ordinances; for to make in himself of twain one new man, so making peace; And that he might reconcile both unto God in one body by the cross, having slain the enmity thereby:"*

Why do we need Jesus? Jesus is the one that brings the peace we need to even start rebuilding our lives. He's our peace and the man that broke the wall of partition between us and God. He abolished the enmity between us and God in His flesh on the cross, so that everything you will ever need to rebuild is paid with His blood. So, without this foundation, it is impossible to rebuild anything.

Are you born again? If you are not, today is your day to make amends and get right with God through Jesus. If you are born again but uncertain of your right standing with God, understand that He is a God of another chance. Let's do it right now. You can say these words:

> Lord Jesus, come in to my life today. I confess You before men that You become my Lord and Savior; I

choose to follow You from now on. I give my life to You. Thank You for Your love for me. Amen

Now that you have a right standing with Jesus, it is time to rebuild the wall of your life, like Nehemiah did, so that the glory can be restored and colors added to your life. Remember, if the foundation be destroyed what can you do? (Psalm 11:3).

Today can be the beginning of great things to come. There are many areas of our lives that need rebuilding and rebranding but it starts here. It does not matter how bad things have gone. Remember, Saul (who was later known as Paul) did many great things and wrote two-third of the New Testament, but he did not start living until the encounter in Acts 9:1-29 (Take some time to read and enjoy the story). As you start this process of rebuilding, the strength from on high will come upon you.

> *"Jesus answered and said unto him, Verily, verily, I say unto thee, Except a man be born again, he cannot see the kingdom of God." (John 3:3)*

WORDS TO PONDER ON...

"For all have sinned"

> *"For all have sinned, and come short of the glory of God; Being justified freely by his grace through the redemption that is in Christ Jesus:" (Romans 3:23-24)*

Did you notice that the passage does not say, "Some have sinned"? It is "all of us". And when we sinned, we fell off the radar of God's glory. We came short of all the benefits that comes with the glory. Thank God for the ministry of reconciliation that restored the lost glory. Do not get frustrated with yourself, the only hope is in Jesus.

ASSIGNMENT

1. Find that glory in Jesus today.
2. Make all the difference with that recovered glory.

Day 7

CONDITION OF THE HEART

"And they said unto me, The remnant that are left of the captivity there in the province are in great affliction and reproach: the wall of Jerusalem also is broken down, and the gates thereof are burned with fire. And it came to pass, when I heard these words, that I sat down and wept, and mourned certain days, and fasted, and prayed before the God of heaven." (Nehemiah 1:3-4)

What an awesome opportunity to rebuild our lives with God so that we can remove every form of reproach! Like Nehemiah, the condition of our heart is very important to God when we plan to rebuild. We can deceive people but not God. The heart of Nehemiah was right with God and he had a pure motive to embark on his journey of rebuilding.

Why is The Condition of Our Heart Important to God?

God does not like to waste time and resources on an unproductive ego. God is not just interested in what we do but also in why we do it. This was the fundamental error in building the tower of Babel.

> *"And they said one to another, Go to, let us make brick, and burn them thoroughly. And they had brick for stone, and slime had they for mortar. And they said, Go to, let us build us a city and a tower, whose top may reach unto heaven; and let us make us a name, lest we be scattered abroad upon the face of the whole earth. And the Lord came down to see the city and the tower, which the children of men builded. And the Lord said, Behold, the people is one, and they have all one language; and this they begin to do: and now nothing will be restrained from them, which they have imagined to do. Go to, let us go down, and there confound their language, that they may not understand one another's speech. So the Lord scattered them abroad from thence upon the face of all the earth: and they left off to build the city." (Genesis 11:3-8)*

The people arose in unity with a great purpose — to build — but there was one problem: the condition of their heart, as revealed by their motive, was ugly. The condition of your heart is not visible but palpable by your motives. The motive for their project was to make a name for themselves, compared to Nehemiah whose heart was broken as a result of the condition of the walls in Jerusalem. What was the result? The Lord came down and destroyed their purpose and the people were scattered. On the other hand, for Nehemiah the king opened up his treasures for what he needed to finish his project of rebuilding. Whenever our heart is right with God and the motive for rebuilding is pure, the provision to rebuild is always readily available without any burden on our shoulders.

Another good example is King Amaziah. It was recorded that he did what was right in the sight of the Lord but not with a perfect heart. *"Amaziah was twenty and five years old when he began to reign, and he reigned twenty and nine years in Jerusalem. And his mother's name was Jehoaddan of Jerusalem. And he did that which was right in the sight of the Lord, but not with a perfect heart." (2 Chronicles 25:1-2)*

The end of king Amaziah, as such, was terrible. Anything not done wholeheartedly is not worth doing at all. The condition of our heart is very important to God, especially when we are soliciting His help to overcome our challenges and limitations.

WORDS TO PONDER ON...

"For the Lord seeth not as man seeth".

> *"But the Lord said unto Samuel, Look not on his countenance, or on the height of his stature; because I have refused him: for the Lord seeth not as man seeth; for man looketh on the outward appearance, but the Lord looketh on the heart." (1 Samuel 16:7)*

It is very easy to fake it with men, you might be able to say all the right things but not with God. Check your motive and get right with God and good things will start happening to you. It is time to put childish behavior aside and grow up.

ASSIGNMENT

1. Align yourself properly with God.
2. Do things for the right reasons.
3. Avoid the mentality of "what is in it for me?"

Day 8

COMMON AREAS OF REBUILDING IN LIFE

"Then I told them of the hand of my God which was good upon me; as also the king's words that he had spoken unto me. And they said, Let us rise up and build. So they strengthened their hands for this good work." (Nehemiah 2:18)

FINDING A CAREER OR REBUILDING ONE

Despite all the woes that came upon the wall of Jerusalem, Nehemiah was able to dream again. Finding a career or rebuilding one requires the ability to dream again. Every house built requires a great deal of planning. In fact, the most important thing about a house is the foundation. The foundation of any hopeful building or rebuilding venture is the ability to DREAM. If the foundation of any house is not solid, the end result is total disaster. (We have seen or heard of many lives lost due to a sudden collapse of such buildings). A career is a dream given to an individual by God. If the devil doesn't attack you about your chosen career, then the career you have chosen is not a threat to his kingdom.

The ability to dream and interpret the dream is very important for you to see your dream realized. In the case of Nehemiah, he had a vision of the end result of his dream and was willing to fight to the end. Another example from the Bible is Joseph (Read Genesis 37:2, 5-9) He was working together with his brothers, feeding the cattle, but felt he was called to something bigger. You might be thinking that life has got to be better than this. Maybe you are saying "I am made for more"; all that feeling is from God as a drive to dream bigger like Joseph. God still gives dreams today!

When God gave Joseph the picture of what his future would look like, guess what? Joseph embraced it and went to work, building the dream into reality. Of course, like Nehemiah, Joseph had five major setbacks on his way to fulfilling his dream (career) and realizing his destiny. Let us take a quick look at what the obstacles were:

1. He was cast into the pit.

2. Sold to the Midianites.

3. Became a slave in a strange land.

4. Went to prison.

5. Forgotten by the people he helped while in prison.

Deuteronomy 28:1,12 tells us that if we diligently hearken to the voice of the Lord, the Lord will open His good treasure to us. Doesn't that look like what Nehemiah got from the king? Of course, Nehemiah got that and much more. The process of building or rebuilding our career begins with our ability to hear and do what the Lord tells us. Think of Nehemiah's prayer when he reminded God of His promises to Israel. From this promise, it looks like God has just given us a blank check and He's telling us to write whatever amount we want on it.

What are the things needed to build or rebuild our career? We shall consider the answers in the next few chapters.

WORDS TO PONDER ON...

"I will pour out my Spirit"

> *"And it shall come to pass afterward, that I will pour out my spirit upon all flesh; and your sons and your daughters shall prophesy, your old men shall dream dreams, your young men shall see visions: And also upon the servants and upon the handmaids in those days will I pour out my spirit." (Joel 2:28-29)*

The Spirit of the Lord is the master planner and builder of any career you might be planning on taking up. That's the reason why He's called the 'Helper'. The Holy Spirit according to Joel 2:28-29 will energize both young and old to dream again—and that includes you. So, pick yourself up and dream again.

ASSIGNMENT

1. Dream again.
2. Be prepared for obstacles.
3. Get into the Word to hear God directly.

Day 9

SEEKING GOD FIRST

There are five things that I identified in Joseph's life that helped him to gain mastery in life. In this chapter, we will discuss one of them and we will touch on the rest in the next four chapters.

WHY SHOULD WE SEEK GOD FIRST?

Joseph sought after God first in all he did and encountered on his way to the throne in Egypt. He put God's interest ahead of his. He sincerely followed the same principle as we find in Matthew 6:33. Matthew 6:33 provides us with us a glimpse into what makes building or rebuilding a career the easiest task to anyone. It encourages us to seek first the Kingdom of God and His righteousness and that EVERY OTHER THING shall be added unto us. That includes your career! *"But seek ye first the kingdom of God, and his righteousness; and all these things shall be added unto you." (Matthew 6:33)*

Joseph trusted God all the way. When he was in the pit, he did not curse God and say "what the heck". He knew God was faithful to His word. When he was sold to the Midianites, though he was getting farther from home, he was moving closer to the fulfillment of his dream. He kept his focus on God who is too faithful to fail. At Potiphar's house, he served faithfully as a slave, knowing that none of the word of God will fall to the ground. He was sent to the prison for refusing to sleep with his boss's wife, because, according to him, he feared God. He accepted to be locked up for the sin he didn't commit while still looking unto God as the author and finisher of his faith. Forgotten by the benefactors that he helped in prison, he kept his focus on God, and like Nehemiah, he sought after God.

WORDS TO PONDER ON...

"We have toiled all night"

> *"And Simon answering said unto him, Master, we have toiled all the night, and have taken nothing: nevertheless at thy word I will let down the net." (Luke 5:5)*

If you have labored and nothing seems to be working, try engaging in Kingdom stewardship. Let Jesus use your boat, and you will find that everything will work in your favor.

ASSIGNMENT

1. Make a list of areas of your life where you want God to be number one.

2. Break down any barrier in your way preventing you from making God your number one.

Day 10

FAVOR FACTOR

"And I said unto the king, If it please the king, and if thy servant have found favour in thy sight, that thou wouldest send me unto Judah, unto the city of my fathers' sepulchres, that I may build it." (Nehemiah 2:5)

WHY FAVOR FACTOR?

Nehemiah asked for the favor of the king, and that made a big difference. Like Nehemiah, we need a dose of God's favor in whatever career path we choose. One day of favor with God in your career is worth more than a lifetime of earnings. When God favors you, it will be difficult for anyone to reject you. Joseph is a typical example of someone that enjoyed God's favor. He went through hell and high water but nothing could take his focus away from the end goal—a throne somewhere. Nehemiah and Joseph are two biblical characters that enjoyed the 'favor factor'.

Nehemiah was a cupbearer for over twenty years without ever displaying a sad countenance. This doesn't mean that the whole of the twenty years had been great for him. In fact, being in captivity alone—and not knowing the time one is ever going to be free—is enough to dampen one's spirit. But not this man. What did Nehemiah and Joseph have in common? Psalms 102:13 gives us a hint. Both men constantly remembered Zion. Their hope and focus were in the wellbeing of Zion. For us to enjoy the constant favor of God, our attention must be on how we can advance the cause of the church of Christ. When God arises and blesses Zion, you will be a beneficiary of such favor.

> *"Thou shalt arise, and have mercy upon Zion: for the time to favour her, yea, the set time, is come. For thy servants take pleasure in her stones, and favour the dust thereof." (Psalms 102:13-14)*

WORDS TO PONDER ON...

"Thou shall be called Hephzibah"

> *"Thou shalt no more be termed Forsaken; neither shall thy land any more be termed Desolate: but thou shalt be called Hephzibah, and thy land Beulah: for the Lord delighteth in thee, and thy land shall be married."(Isaiah 62:4)*

The Bible calls God's favorite Hephzibah (God's delight). When the favor of God shines on you, you will no longer be termed 'forsaken', neither will your land be desolate any longer, and your rebuilding effort shall be called Beulah (plenteous).

ASSIGNMENT

1. Ask yourself: What am I doing for the advancement of the Kingdom?

2. Identify an area where you can be useful for God.

Day 11

POWER OF DILIGENCE

"So built we the wall; and all the wall was joined together unto the half thereof: for the people had a mind to work." (Nehemiah 4:6)

The force of diligence is the constant and earnest effort to accomplish that which is undertaken. Building or rebuilding a career requires a lot of diligence. Nehemiah had a force of diligence working in his life and he cultivated the same in his men. His men took away their clothes only to shower; they had tool in one hand and weapon in the other. The same could be said of Joseph. He was an epitome of diligence. It was so obvious in his life that wherever he got into, they made him the supervisor immediately. In the realm of highfliers, favor brings you in but it is diligence that keeps you in. The promise of getting into God's good treasure is based on the premise of diligently obeying the instructions from the Bible. For us to excel in any chosen career, the force of diligence must dominate our being completely. Let us look at the areas in which these men were diligent:

1. They were diligent in purpose, as both men sought after God.
2. They were diligent in panting after righteousness.
3. They were diligent in paying attention to what God said.
4. They were diligent in prayer.
5. They were diligent in praising God.
6. They were diligent in encouraging others and preaching the word.
7. They were diligent in promoting the Kingdom of God.
8. They were diligent in partnership.

Pursuing any career—whether you are building or rebuilding—requires a force of diligence. Diligence in all these areas is a 'must' to excel and build an enduring career.

> *"Seest thou a man diligent in his business? he shall stand before kings; he shall not stand before mean men." (Proverbs 22:29)*

WORDS TO PONDER ON...

"The thought of the diligent"

> *"The thoughts of the diligent tend only to plenteousness; but of every one that is hasty only to want." (Proverbs 21:5)*

The force of diligence is so efficient that it causes the thoughts of the diligent—just their thoughts; not their actions—to tend only to plenteousness. Let that force of diligence begin to work for you from today.

ASSIGNMENT

1. In what areas do you lack the force of diligence?
2. How can you develop this force?
3. What accountability mechanism do you have in place?

Day 12

POWER OF PERSEVERANCE

"So we laboured in the work: and half of them held the spears from the rising of the morning till the stars appeared. Likewise at the same time said I unto the people, Let everyone with his servant lodge within Jerusalem, that in the night they may be a guard to us, and labour on the day." (Nehemiah 4:21-22)

WHY PERSEVERANCE?

Perseverance is much needed in our world today. The world we live in now is the drive-through world, where everything must happen in an instant. From food processing to Internet intervention, everything is on steroids; so, if something is not happening now, there is hardly any patience for it to develop.

Perseverance is patience and power packaged together for a greater benefit. For Nehemiah, it took only fifty-two days from the start to finish of rebuilding the wall, although the amount of opposition they encountered would have made those days seem like eternity.

Joseph even persevered the more; he was seventeen years old when he dreamt and became a prime minister by the age of thirty. That leaves us with a thirteen-year period that we have to account for in his life. If he had given up in his twelfth year of waiting, it would have been all over. We don't know how long he spent in the pit, but surely it was long enough to find a buyer.

When people die, typically they are buried in a six-foot pit but Joseph was dumped into something deeper. He was later transferred to the Midianites—a people that he never knew; people that do not have covenant with the God of the Hebrews. He spent eleven years in slavery at the house of Potiphar and then two years in prison before he finally became the prime minister in Egypt. Everyone who wants to excel in a chosen career must develop perseverance. As the saying goes, "Rome was not built in a day", so also your career cannot be established in a day. Building or rebuilding any career requires a boatload of patience, and patience must have its perfect work for anything to materialize. Favor gets you in, diligence keeps you in and perseverance is the tool that gets you focused on the end result. Joseph stayed in because he persevered when the enemy turned the furnace up. To build or rebuild you need a boatload of patience as we are admonished in James 1:2-4: *"My brethren, count it all joy when ye fall into divers temptations; Knowing this, that the trying of your faith worketh patience. But let patience have her perfect work, that ye may be perfect and entire, wanting nothing."*

WORDS TO PONDER ON...

"Strengthened with all might"

> *"Strengthened with all might, according to his glorious power, unto all patience and longsuffering with joyfulness." (Colossians 1:11)*

Sometimes it takes the might of the Almighty to help us endure to the end. There's joy coming in the morning, but it will require you to endure the weeping which may last through the night (Psalm 30:5).

ASSIGNMENT

1. What does perseverance mean to you?
2. How do you develop it?
3. What is the evidence of this trait in your career?

Day 13

POWER OF PRAYER

"And it came to pass, when I heard these words, that I sat down and wept, and mourned certain days, and fasted, and prayed before the God of heaven," (Nehemiah 1:4)

WHY PRAYER?

Prayer is simply talking to God based on what He promised in His word. Nehemiah did pray numerous times reminding God of His covenant relationship with the children of Israel and what He promised to do for them. God responded to Nehemiah every time, not because he was a special guy, but because he prayed God's word every time.

Prayer can also be defined as a simple way of telling the mountains to get out of your way. Joseph, our great example, must have prayed a lot to be able to overcome all the opposition that came along his way. You may want to ask, how are we sure that Joseph prayed since it was never recorded directly in the Bible? Let me show you how I know that he was a great prayer warrior. Do you remember the biblical story of a man called Daniel? Remember that the king had a dream and wanted it to be reproduced and interpreted. The king commanded that all the magicians and astrologers be put to death if no one could interpret the dream. But Daniel, a man in whom the Spirit of God dwelled, asked the king for time to pray and enquire from God and he was able to reveal the dream and the interpretation to the king (Daniel 2:14-19). The Bible tells us that the secret of the Lord is with them that fear Him. For Joseph to dream and narrate the dream to his family—even when the narration of the dream would bring him a lot of trouble—he was a praying man. Joseph interpreted at least three dreams which eventually took him from the prison to palace.

Building or rebuilding a career requires you to dream—which is the foundation—and to correctly interpret the dream requires some time in prayer. Joseph was a beautiful example of demonstrating these qualities—seeking God first, experiencing the favor factor, being diligent, persevering, and praying. If you want to build or rebuild anything for posterity sake, these qualities are very much needed. As you build or rebuild your career, may the Lord make His face to shine upon you.

WORDS TO PONDER ON...

"Whosoever shall say to this mountain"

"For verily I say unto you, That whosoever shall say unto this mountain, Be thou removed, and be thou cast into the sea; and shall not doubt in his heart, but shall believe that those things which he saith shall come to pass; he shall have whatsoever he saith. Therefore I say unto you, What things soever ye desire, when ye pray, believe that ye receive them, and ye shall have them." (Mark 11:23-24)

When you speak to a mountain in your prayers, what do you tell the mountain? "Be thou removed and be cast in the sea." When you say that without a DOUBT in your heart, answers come steadily.

ASSIGNMENT

1. Begin to dream or dream again for the career of your choice.
2. Develop the habit of knowing what God says in His word about you.
3. Develop a prayer lifestyle by praying what God says in His word.
4. Pray early and always.

Day 14

BUILDING OR REBUILDING A RELATIONSHIP

"Then I told them of the hand of my God which was good upon me; as also the king's words that he had spoken unto me. And they said, Let us rise up and build. So they strengthened their hands for this good work." (Nehemiah 2:18)

Relationship is like building or rebuilding a house—building, if it is a new relationship; rebuilding if it is an old and/or broken relationship. Relationship happens on a plurality of levels—establishing a friendship, dating, engaging a business partner or developing intimacy with a family member—whatever involves two or more people interacting with each other; and they all operate with the same patterns, with slight variations. For the purpose of this devotional, let us focus our attention on the marital relationship—from dating to marriage.

The absence of God in a relationship is like building or rebuilding a house on sand. In our opening verse, Nehemiah told the people about how the hand of God had been good upon him and of the king's word spoken to him. This statement establishes two of the most important foundations upon which every relationship must be built: the presence of God's influence and being guarded and guided by the word of the King (God)—the Bible. With these two elements present, a relationship is off to a good start.

Another important factor to be considered in any relationship, especially when rebuilding it, is the condition of the heart of both individuals. If we engage in a relationship for the wrong reasons, the outcome will not be good. God loves relationships—in fact, He invented it. He instituted both the relationship that exists between Him and man, and the relationship between a man and a woman.

In order to talk about building or rebuilding a relationship, we must consult the manufacturer's manual, which is the Bible. Deuteronomy 28:1,12 tells us that if we diligently hearken to voice of the Lord—which is the word of God (the relationship manual)—then all we need to build or rebuild is available at our fingertips. The Lord promises to open His good treasures to us and the needed materials will be made available so that we can build the life that we will love. Let us look at how God put the invention of a marital relationship together.

RELEASED BY COUNSEL

From Genesis 1, it is very clear that God created all things for His pleasure, including man (male and female). God spoke and things came into existence - until the twenty-sixth verse: "and God said, "Let us make man in our image"." From this statement it is obvious that man was made from and by counsel; God consulted the Godhead. Likewise, for any man to establish any good relationship, it has to be built on good and godly counsel. Many relationships fail because they are not subjected to adequate godly counsel. Man was made by counsel and should live by counsel.

THE BLESSEDNESS OF A RELATIONSHIP

After the creation of man, God pronounced certain blessings upon them.

> *"And God blessed them, and God said unto them, Be fruitful, and multiply, and replenish the earth, and subdue it: and have dominion over the fish of the sea, and over the fowl of the air, and over every living thing that moveth upon the earth." (Genesis 1:28)*

As such, for any relationship to be functional, these five blessings must be operational. The relationship must make room for fruitfulness, must be able to replicate itself, must find a way to invigorate itself, defined authority must be established and each individual involved must excel. Conflicts ensue if any of these elements is missing. In fact, the wall of Jerusalem broke down when these blessings of the Lord ceased upon the people.

REAWAKENED BY THE SPIRIT

God created man in Genesis 1:26 and blessed them. In Genesis 2:7, we see how He formed man of the dust of the ground. These two verses offer a parallel for a man to be functional in a relationship: He or she must be formed by God (born again) and the breath of God (Holy Spirit) must come into him or her, before he or she can have a life worth living. In a marital relationship, if both parties are not reawakened by the Spirit, the foundation becomes faulty. To build or rebuild like Nehemiah did, the Spirit of God must take the center stage.

REPOSITIONED FOR ABUNDANCE

When God created man, everything he needed was provided for. Genesis 2:8,15 reveal that God planted a garden eastward in Eden, and there he put man whom He had formed. Thus, God repositioned man for divine provision. What did God provide for man? Accommodation and a job. These two are equally needed to develop man's character and sense of responsibility.

> *"And the Lord God planted a garden eastward in Eden; and there he put the man whom he had formed. And the Lord God took the man, and put him into the garden of Eden to dress it and to keep it." (Genesis 2:8, 15)*

RELATIONSHIP BY OBEDIENCE

In any relationship, if everyone obeys basic and simple instructions, the relationship will be a blissful heaven-on-earth experience. A defined line of authority and accountability is much needed in a relationship. God planted the tree of the knowledge of good and evil in the garden, not to tempt us, but to prepare mankind for what He had in stock for them (Genesis 2:16-17).

Every blessing that God has for us becomes accessible by a simple act of obedience. It is all about obedience! When we obey God and each other, things work well with us. If every married couple would abide by and obey the vows made to each other on their wedding day, a divorce court would not be needed. What this means therefore is that whether you are building or rebuilding a relationship, OBEDIENCE is key!

REFOCUS ON GOD'S PROVISION

Building or rebuilding a relationship begins with the right motives and looking in the right places for God to begin the work of bringing a partner or restoring a broken relationship. For singles, separated spouses or divorcees, God attests that it is not good for you to be alone.

> *"And the Lord God said, It is not good that the man should be alone; I will make him an help meet for him. And Adam gave names to all cattle, and to the fowl of the air, and to every beast of the field; but for Adam there was not found an help meet for him." (Genesis 2:18, 20)*

What Adam could not find amongst the animals, God can provide if we look to Him. Nehemiah looked up to God for all the supplies and support he needed and was able to rebuild successfully.

REMEDY FOR THE BEST RESULT

If God is the foundation of a relationship, it will last forever. The main problem in building or rebuilding a relationship is that God is often not part of the equation. We tend to be too busy trying to figure things out on our own, jumping from one dating service to another. Of course, there's nothing wrong with using a dating service, but my point remains that we need to let God help us. He set a pattern for us with Adam. He caused a deep sleep to fall upon Adam—he must have been very busy trying to find the right 'Eve' which God was yet to create.

> *"And the Lord God caused a deep sleep to fall upon Adam, and he slept: and he took one of his ribs, and closed up the flesh instead thereof; And the rib, which the Lord God had taken from man, made he a woman, and brought her unto the man." (Genesis 2:21-22).*

In building or rebuilding a relationship, there are times that you will have to let God put you to sleep; and, certainly, the result will be everything you want. Let God do it; He will guide you aright.

IT WILL BE EVIDENT WHEN HE OR SHE COMES

"And the rib, which the Lord God had taken from man, made he a woman, and brought her unto the man. And Adam said, This is now bone of my bones, and flesh of my flesh: she shall be called Woman, because she was taken out of Man." (Genesis 2:22-23)

When God is involved, the result will be spectacular. That peculiar person you are looking for, though far or near, only God can direct your paths to cross. Most importantly, when he or she comes, you will know without any shadow of doubt that that is the person meant for you. So, when building or rebuilding a relationship, let God be the only contractor and builder.

MARRIAGE IS THE FINAL RESULT

"Therefore shall a man leave his father and his mother, and shall cleave unto his wife: and they shall be one flesh. And they were both naked, the man and his wife, and were not ashamed." (Genesis 22:24-25)

The goal of building or rebuilding a relationship (in the context in which we have discussed so far) is to end up in a meaningful marriage or the restoration of the married individuals. God's instruction to us is that a man (or woman) must leave his father and mother—which, on its own, is a big subject beyond the scope of this book. But, having said that, there must be a 'leaving' in every sense. Most importantly, in building or rebuilding a relationship, there is a need for absolute transparency. The Bible says they were both naked and were not ashamed—free to talk about everything that could surprise the other party without shame or fear.

What are the things needed to build or rebuild our relationship? We shall consider the answers in the next few chapters.

WORDS TO PONDER ON...

"Prepare Thy work without"

> *"Prepare thy work without, and make it fit for thyself in the field; and afterwards build thine house." (Proverbs 24:27).*

God wants us to depend on Him. At the same time, we have to do what He tells us to do—and that's where the work comes in. For us to build or rebuild successfully, we must have the understanding of working with God and each other throughout the process. The above stated guidelines require being diligent for the house to be built.

ASSIGNMENT

1. Develop a stronger relationship with God.
2. Develop the ability to hear God clearly.
3. Develop the obedience required to follow God.
4. Develop the satisfaction in taking God's word as the final authority.

*If you are interested in attending our Interdenominational Singles' Summit, please contact us for details.

Day 15

WISDOM

"And I arose in the night, I and some few men with me; neither told I any man what my God had put in my heart to do at Jerusalem: neither was there any beast with me, save the beast that I rode upon." (Nehemiah 2:12)

WHY WISDOM?

There are five things that I identified from God's Word that will help us to build or rebuild a great marriage or relationship and that will afford us the stability we need in life. In this chapter, we will discuss one and the rest in the subsequent four chapters.

Wisdom is the knowledge of what is true or right with a just judgment of acting on the knowledge. According to the dictionary, it is the correct application of what you know. The Bible rightly describes wisdom as the principal thing (Proverbs 4:7); it can only take the wisdom of God to understand any human being and that is a mystery on its own. The problem we encounter in building or rebuilding a relationship is that we want to figure out everything on our own terms and that alone poses a great danger to the survivability of any relationship. There is a great need to depend on the wisdom of God to engage the other person from a different background, upbringing and financial status—just to mention a few. For you to get the proper perspective of your partner you need wisdom and it only comes from God—the more reason why God must be the foundation of your relationship.

Wisdom does not come alone when invited to participate in any relationship. Proverbs 9:1 tells us that wisdom is a builder who builds on seven pillars. "Wisdom hath builded her house, she hath hewn out her seven pillars." When your house is supported by pillars, it will be quite difficult to bring it down. What are the seven pillars that wisdom brings? Bearing in mind that seven is a symbol of perfection, embracing wisdom brings your relationship into perfect unity. The seven pillars are:

1. Prudence—Doing the right thing;
2. Knowledge—knowing what is true/right;
3. Discretion—forethought and acting based on conviction and according to truth, to be discreetly different;
4. Counsel—purpose with unity;
5. Sound judgment—decision making, ability to determine right from wrong;
6. Understanding—applied knowledge;
7. Power—the ability or rate of getting things done.

With all these present to guide you, then you are on your way to wonderfully building or rebuilding your relationship. It thus becomes very obvious why King Solomon considered wisdom as the principal thing to have.

Where can we get wisdom? The Bible tells us that Jesus is the wisdom of God (1 Corinthians 1:24); so when Jesus comes in, wisdom comes in.

WORDS TO PONDER ON...

"By wisdom the Lord…"

> *"The Lord by wisdom hath founded the earth; by understanding hath he established the heavens." (Proverbs 3:19)*

God Himself required wisdom to build the earth in which we now live. What a beautiful world! The Bible says everything God created was good—why? Because the wisdom of the Lord was the architect. Building or rebuilding a relationship requires it; so, please subscribe to this wisdom. If even God needed it to build, then who are we?

ASSIGNMENT

1. Seek after wisdom.
2. Do what wisdom tells you.
3. Ask God for it.

Day 16

POWER OF LOVE

"That Hanani, one of my brethren, came, he and certain men of Judah; and I asked them concerning the Jews that had escaped, which were left of the captivity, and concerning Jerusalem." (Nehemiah 1:2)

WHY LOVE?

Everything works by love. Even faith that moves the mountains operates effectively and efficiently by the power of love. Nehemiah's love for the people back in Jerusalem became the driving force that propelled him to God's presence for a dialogue that resulted in restoration. Like wisdom, love also has many facets or characteristics that amplify its necessity in building and rebuilding relationships.

Why love? Love never fails! Every other thing will fail and be done away with, but love remains constant. In fact, it takes all of God to love someone because God is love! Let us look at the attributes of love that makes love very important in building or rebuilding a relationship:

> *"Charity [love] suffereth long, and is kind; charity envieth not; charity vaunteth not itself, is not puffed up, Doth not behave itself unseemly, seeketh not her own, is not easily provoked, thinketh no evil; Rejoiceth not in iniquity, but rejoiceth in the truth; Beareth all things, believeth all things, hopeth all things, endureth all things. Charity never faileth: but whether there be prophecies, they shall fail; whether there be tongues, they shall cease; whether there be knowledge, it shall vanish away." (1 Corinthians 13:4-8)*

- Love suffers long. Love gives you the ability to develop longsuffering, which is the combination of power and patience. Jesus did not quit at the first instance of opposition, and neither should you. You should not walk out when things are not convenient for you.
- Love is kind. In any relationship, where kindness is often demonstrated towards one another, the result is bliss.
- Love does not envy. Envy is the most potent force that has broken relationships and has limited some individuals from reaching out to bring someone else into their lives.
- Love vaunts not itself. It does not speak vaingloriously; it considers the other person's feeling and perspectives.
- Love is not puffed up. It is not proud and doesn't look down on others.
- Love doesn't behave unseemly. In fact, herein lies the solution to most problems in building or rebuilding a relationship. If everyone involved would just behave according to biblical standards, most of the problems in relationships would have been solved.

- Love doesn't seek her own. There is probably no other place where selfish behavior hurts more than in relationships. When we become selfish and allow 'I' to replace 'we' in any relationship, the end has come for that relationship.

- Love is not easily provoked. It helps us to develop patience and tolerance for each other. Anger is very destructive and love is the only antidote.

- Love thinks no evil. Our thoughts constitute an integral part of our lives, especially in our relationship. When we don't think evil of one another, misinterpretation in a relationship is kept to the minimum.

- Love doesn't rejoice in iniquity. When you feel happy because your ex is in trouble, reconciliation becomes more difficult. Rather, love rejoices in the truth. In fact, the moment we stop believing in each other, love stops working. Only the truth sets free.

- Love rejoices in freedom - allowing each other to be who they are meant to be without any fear of intimidation.

- Love bears, believes, hopes, and endures all things! No doubt, this can only be done by God. When we allow God to work in us, with us, and through us, all things are possible in our relationship.

All these attributes make love failure-proof and when it is allowed to be demonstrated, no relationship can fail and the process to build or rebuild becomes very sweet and easy.

WORDS TO PONDER ON...

"The first and second commandment is love."

> *"Jesus said unto him, Thou shalt love the Lord thy God with all thy heart, and with all thy soul, and with all thy mind. This is the first and great commandment. And the second is like unto it, Thou shalt love thy neighbour as thyself." (Matthew 22:37-39)*

Jesus said concerning loving the Lord and loving one's neighbor: "on these two commandments hang all the law and the prophets." (Matthew 22:40). In other words, everything in the Bible works by love.

ASSIGNMENT

1. What is love to you?
2. Determine to treat your spouse right, not fair.
3. Develop self-sacrifice.
4. Be grateful always.

Day 17

THE POWER OF FORGIVENESS

"Let thine ear now be attentive, and thine eyes open, that thou mayest hear the prayer of thy servant, which I pray before thee now, day and night, for the children of Israel thy servants, and confess the sins of the children of Israel, which we have sinned against thee: both I and my father's house have sinned." (Nehemiah 1:6)

WHY FORGIVENESS?

Nehemiah sat down and wept. He mourned certain days because of the sins committed by the children of Israel. He quickly realized the reason they were in the predicament of ruins: they had deviated from God to serve other gods. God is a jealous Being, due to His love for the children of Israel. The problem with our relationships is that we often cross each other's path, and when that happens we become hurt and resentful. Taking a cue from Nehemiah, the first thing he did was to focus his attention back to God in sincere and heartfelt repentance; and forgiveness was granted in an instant for many years of transgressions.

When building a relationship, it is essential to know that we will offend each other and forgiveness is a 'must'; otherwise it will be a futile effort cultivating any relationship. Rebuilding a relationship is not an easy task, either. It begins with a commitment and willingness to sit down with each other—not to complain, but to confess to one another our faults without any judgmental attitude—and that is where forgiveness begins.

The Bible instructs us to confess our faults to each other and then we can pray for one another.

> *"Confess your faults one to another, and pray one for another, that ye may be healed. The effectual fervent prayer of a righteous man availeth much." (James 5:16)*

Prayer should not precede confession. The reason we are not seeing as many healed relationships as possible is because we are putting the cart before the horse; healing will be available if there is a sincere confession of faults followed by prayers. Find out where you have hurt each other, detect why and how you both allowed things to get out of hand. In certain instances, it might be necessary to have a third party's intervention, such as your pastor or a counselor.

It is very important to know that opportunities to offend each other will always be present, but we need to know what to do in those moments of weakness. The Bible even says that it is normal to be upset but we must do everything possible—of course, relying on the Holy Spirit and grace of God—not to allow that anger to make us sin. *"Be ye angry, and sin not: let not the sun go down upon your wrath: Neither give place to the devil." (Ephesians 4:26-27)*

The instruction in that verse that I have personally struggled with is not allowing the sun to go down on one's wrath – because, when we do, we are giving a place to the devil. I am still praying for grace in this regard, and so are millions of other people struggling with this. So, you are not alone; the grace of God is available. If we can do these things, building or rebuilding a relationship will be possible and as a result we will develop a frictionless relationship.

WORDS TO PONDER ON...

"If any man have a quarrel against you..." (or you against them)

> *"Forbearing one another, and forgiving one another, if any man have a quarrel against any: even as Christ forgave you, so also do ye." (Colossians 3:13)*

Some of us find it very easy to forgive friends but when it comes to our spouse, then forgiveness becomes impossible. But looking at the biblical phrase above, remember that 'any man' includes your partner! Christ is our perfect example; as He has forgiven us despite what He went through for our sakes on the cross, it doesn't matter how many times or what type of offense you have committed, He is always standing tall ready to forgive.

ASSIGNMENT

1. Identify areas in which you are struggling to forgive.
2. Resolve to make God the focus of your relationship.
3. Since forgiveness is not a choice, but something that must be done for your own good, begin to think of grievances that you have to let go.

Day 18

UNITED PRAYER

"Then said I unto them, Ye see the distress that we are in, how Jerusalem lieth waste, and the gates thereof are burned with fire: come, and let us build up the wall of Jerusalem, that we be no more a reproach." (Nehemiah 2:17)

WHY PRAYER?

Prayer is simply communicating with the Almighty. In the context of relationship therefore, this refers to how we communicate our findings after engaging in dialogue with each other. Confessing our faults is just one part of the equation. As discussed in the previous chapter, confession must precede prayer for divine healing to take place. When we confess to one another and pray, then it is time to make further commitment to do whatever the word of God tells us.

Nehemiah was faced with a daunting task of rebuilding the

wall that had been in ruins for at least twenty years. Similarly, sometimes our collapsed relationship might seem as daunting a task. Our commitment to do whatever the Word tells us is the way to see our rebuilding effort becoming fruitful.

What does the Word say about how to pray?

> *"Be careful for nothing; but in everything by prayer and supplication with thanksgiving let your requests be made known unto God. And the peace of God, which passeth all understanding, shall keep your hearts and minds through Christ Jesus." (Philippians 4:6-7)*

Here, the Scripture reveals to us how to pray; it tells us to be careful for nothing—in other words, we should not look at how bad the situation has become—but in prayer, tell God what outcomes you would like to see, calling those things that be not as though they were! Instantly, you will experience the peace that so passes all understanding that your understanding would not be able to comprehend what is about to happen; you will need to see it with spiritual eyes. It is divine healing indeed because the dramatic change that will take place might be unexplainable.

Building or rebuilding a relationship requires constant and fervent prayer. The scripture tells us that two are better than one and a threefold cord is not easily broken. Two shall have a better reward for their labor (Ecclesiastes 4:9-12). Friend, that includes prayers! One shall chase a thousand and two, ten thousand—what an exploit! The main reason why the devil loves to destroy relationships or discourage people from engaging in them is simply because of the power of two people in prayer. Look at this mystery of two again in Matthew 18:20:

> *"For where two or three are gathered together in my name, there am I in the midst of them." (Matthew 18:20)*

Think about this for a moment. How do we start our prayer? Mostly we say, "In the name of Jesus". So, when two in a relationship say that name, the devil trembles because the presence of Jesus is immediately invoked! That's when we see Satan falling! The war that hell is waging on relationships in this dispensation is to stop us from using the power of united prayer to attack his kingdom.

WORDS TO PONDER ON...

"Produce your cause..."

> *"Produce your cause, saith the Lord; bring forth your strong reasons, saith the King of Jacob." (Isaiah 41:21)*

God is very much interested in hearing from us. In the above verse, the Lord asks us to produce our cause. When you go to court, you present your case to the judge through your attorney. The good news here is that Jesus is your advocate and God is the judge; so bring forth your strong reason and you will be justified and your relationship shall be restored.

ASSIGNMENT

1. Accept that the real enemy is not your spouse.
2. Confront that enemy with a unified front.
3. Have faith in God for divine intervention and healing.

Day 19

POWER OF FASTING

"And it came to pass, when I heard these words, that I sat down and wept, and mourned certain days, and fasted, and prayed before the God of heaven," (*Nehemiah 1:4*)

WHY FASTING?

Nehemiah, our great example, used a combination of the different principles previously discussed to get the rebuilding project started. He applied wisdom in approaching the king and the people (wisdom); he loved the people enough not to leave the city of Jerusalem in ruins (love); he asked God for forgiveness of all their sins (forgiveness); and he wept and mourned in united prayer with the people for the healing of their land (united prayer).

Nehemiah also consecrated himself with fasting. When fasting is done right, it brings down the invincible power of God. We have seen how Nehemiah engaged in the type of fast that God ordained and how he became the world-renowned repairer of the breach of his time.

Why fasting? Matthew 17:21 reveals that some problem might not respond to prayer alone, but when fasting is coupled with prayer, it produces tremendous result! The verse says "howbeit this kind doesn't go out but by prayer and fasting." Whatever your relationship or marital situation might be—a difficult partner, an anger issue, poor financial management, an absentee father or mother, whatever it is—it must yield to a fasting and prayer combination.

Now, think about it. The Bible says that one will chase a thousand and two ten thousand; when fasting is added to that then it becomes explosive.

I know the question that may be going through your mind: What is the proper way to do the God-kind of fasting? It was described at the beginning of this book, but it won't hurt if we go over it again. Isaiah 58 gives a good look at the kind of fast that the Lord chooses:

> *"Is not this the fast that I have chosen? to loose the bands of wickedness, to undo the heavy burdens, and to let the oppressed go free, and that ye break every yoke? Is it not to deal thy bread to the hungry, and that thou bring the poor that are cast out to thy house? when thou seest the naked, that thou cover him; and that thou hide not thyself from thine own flesh?" (6-7)*

The day of fasting is a day to loose the bands of wickedness, to undo heavy burdens, to let the oppressed go free, and to break every yoke, to take care of the poor, cover the naked and do good unto them of the household of faith.

What Does All of This Mean?

It means that fasting is not just about going hungry but rather a time to pray, and seek the advancement of the Kingdom of God. As you prepare to build or rebuild your relationship, consecrating yourself in fasting and prayer for a productive result, I pray for you and with you that there shall be an everlasting solution. God is the same yesterday, today and forever; if He answered back then, He must answer now.

Remember the experience of Jesus after His forty-day fast? He returned in the power of the Spirit after he had fasted forty days. He literally received strength to rebuild the pathway of salvation back to God. When you fast, you are positioning yourself for an unusual strength to build afresh or rebuild that which the enemy has destroyed. The scriptures says,

"looking unto Jesus the author and the finisher of our faith." (Hebrews 12:2).

WORDS TO PONDER ON...

"With God all things are possible"

"But Jesus beheld them, and said unto them, With men this is impossible; but with God all things are possible." (Matthew 19:26)

Jesus is looking at your relationship today and saying to you: This might look impossible, but when you add me (GOD), who has the awesome power to make all hurt better and give you a brand new heart to love again, ALL THINGS are possible! As you believe, within the next few days or weeks, you shall be singing "Hosanna in the highest" Amen.

ASSIGNMENT

1. Try fasting, it works.
2. Do the kind of fasting that God approves.
3. Find out in the Bible the benefits of fasting.
4. Make a list of two or three people in the Bible that engaged in fasting.

Day 20

BUILDING OR REBUILDING A FAMILY

"And they said unto me, The remnant that are left of the captivity there in the province are in great affliction and reproach: the wall of Jerusalem also is broken down, and the gates thereof are burned with fire." (Nehemiah 1:3)

Every father or mother wants to be a great parent for their children – just as God is to us. We all want to be like Him. Why? He's a parent with solid character and that's why when we are called the sons or daughters of God, our heart rejoices greatly simply because we identify with Him. We become very proud when we hear that our children look just like us. The same is true with our God. Being happy parents and having wonderful children begins with a good and solid family structure. This is the reason God instituted and cares for the family.

Nehemiah realized that the family unit in Jerusalem had disintegrated completely and, as a result, the wall was completely broken down. Today in our society, the same is true and the result is a broken down society and massive incarceration among the youths, especially among the minorities and single parents. As such, like Nehemiah, we must be determined to build or rebuild areas of our lives in ruins and to reinforce areas that are doing well.

A family is an integral part of any healthy society and that's the reason why the devil is all out to destroy it—not yours alone but all families. Let us look at the very first family that God put together. It was attacked by the devil, and that attack brought God out of rest. God rested after He finished creation, but after this attack on the family unit, God began a process that would bring man back to his rightful inheritance. In the previous chapters we have considered restoring our personal relationship with God, getting the condition of our heart right and restoring our marital relationship. This chapter focuses on building or rebuilding our families and raising children in the way of the Lord.

The reason we must guard, build or rebuild our families is in two folds. The first is in Exodus 23:26, which says "There shall nothing cast their young, nor be barren, in thy land: the number of thy days I will fulfil." This simply shows that something is actually attempting to make the people cast their young—and this goes beyond dying. There are many things trying to disrupt the future of our children. For example, a seventeen-year-old sentenced to life imprisonment is as good as a wasted destiny.

The second reason is in Psalms 127:3-5, which says,

> *"Lo, children are an heritage of the Lord: and the fruit of the womb is his reward. As arrows are in the hand of a mighty man; so are children of the youth. Happy is the man that hath his quiver full of them: they shall not be ashamed, but they shall speak with the enemies in the gate."*

You will agree with me that the devil hates what God loves. As such, the devil is out to destroy the man with the quiver holding the arrows for God. This is the reason why wives should pray for their husbands on behalf of their children.

How do we begin the process of building or rebuilding our families? Since God is the inventor of the family, we need to consult the owner's manual in order to get the right perspective on how to build or fix it. What are the things we need to make our families work? The answer is not far-fetched, as we shall see in the next chapter.

WORDS TO PONDER ON...

"You will be saved and your household..."

> *"And they said, Believe on the Lord Jesus Christ, and thou shalt be saved, and thy house." (Acts 16:31)*

God is not only interested in you but in your entire household—what a thoughtful God we serve! When you come to God, He expects you to show up with your family.

ASSIGNMENT

1. Find out what's going on in your family.
2. Know your children on an individual basis.
3. Attend a seminar to make you a better father or mother.

Day 21

STABLE HOMES

"Then Eliashib the high priest rose up with his brethren the priests, and they builded the sheep gate; they sanctified it, and set up the doors of it; even unto the tower of Meah they sanctified it, unto the tower of Hananeel." (Nehemiah 3:1)

WHY STABLE HOMES?

The need for a stable home, where children could be safely raised, cannot be over-emphasized. Let us look at the first family; when their home became unstable, the unthinkable happened. When they were evicted from the Garden of Eden, due to the fault of the parents, the home environment became unhealthy to raise children in. Of the two children they had, one was murdered and the other became a vagabond and a fugitive as a result of the first ever foreclosure recorded in the history of mankind.

Circumstances beyond our control can force us to lose our homes, but we must learn not to bite more than we can chew, when it comes to buying a house. If these children had been raised in the Garden of Eden, the result, perhaps, might have been different. Genesis 4:25-26 shows that they had another son named Seth, and from that generation onwards, men began to call upon the name of the Lord. "And Adam knew his wife again; and she bare a son, and called his name Seth: For God, said she, hath appointed me another seed instead of Abel, whom Cain slew. And to Seth, to him also there was born a son; and he called his name Enos: then began men to call upon the name of the Lord." The family altar was reestablished and he grew to be a great man.

Another good example was King David (2 Samuel 11:1-2). During the time when kings went to war, he decided to stay back and relax. That old adage that an idle hand is the devil's workshop became true concerning him. He committed adultery with Bathsheba, whom he later married. His children heard and saw what their father did, and they replicated the same—only worse! Ammon raped his half-sister and was murdered by Absalom. Absalom slept with his father's concubines on the rooftop. Can a household be any more unstable? Whenever I read their stories, I ask myself, "where were the mothers to these kids?" I don't have an answer, but a good guess will be that they were probably busy fighting for their spots on the king's bedroom roster. For whatever reason, David and his wives failed their children. Though a great king, he failed where it mattered most!

Isaac and Rebecca were horrible parents as well. They literally destroyed their two kids by their selfishness and favoritism. The two kids ended up as sworn enemies to each other—what a shame! Joshua made it clear that as for him and his household they would serve the Lord. The need for a stable home to give our children the best opportunity to thrive is very important. Whether you are building or rebuilding, start by securing a good and stable household where dad and mom are both present to raise godly children.

WORDS TO PONDER ON...

"As for me and my house..."

> *"And if it seem evil unto you to serve the Lord, choose you this day whom ye will serve; whether the gods which your fathers served that were on the other side of the flood, or the gods of the Amorites, in whose land ye dwell: but as for me and my house, we will serve the Lord." (Joshua 24:15)*

It is the responsibility of the father to take the lead in the family. Joshua made a declaration that he would serve the Lord. His family knew where he stood when it came to the things of God. The father is the head and the mother the neck; they must work together to lead their children in the right path.

ASSIGNMENT

1. Determine if your home is stable.
2. Do you have a church home?
3. Do you have a family altar?
4. Do you talk to your kids?

Day 22

BUILDING GODLY CHARACTER

"And I arose in the night, I and some few men with me; neither told I any man what my God had put in my heart to do at Jerusalem: neither was there any beast with me, save the beast that I rode upon." (Nehemiah 2:12)

WHY GODLY CHARACTER?

Nehemiah was a man of impeccable and exemplary character. This was obvious in all his dealings with the children of Israel. It is obvious, from the above verse, that despite the fact that he had not revealed his intentions on why he came back to Jerusalem, few men of high repute followed him and were willing to risk even their own lives.

In a spiritual sense, God is our father. Genesis 1:26-27 tells us that God created man in His own image and likeness, male and female He created them. God is a man of character, and that must be our gold standard. There are several attributes of God, and it will be quite difficult to match them all. Hence in Ephesians 4:13, Paul exhorts us to attain the unity of faith, and the knowledge of the Son of God, unto a complete or perfect man, unto the measure of the stature of the fullness of Christ in our godly character.

How do we do this? There are a few scriptures to guide us:

1. God keeps His word (Numbers 23:19). Likewise, we must do our very best to keep our word.

2. God is truthful (Ephesians 4:25). Likewise we must do our very best to be truthful and not encourage our kids to lie on our behalf.

3. God is dependable (Psalms 15:4).

4. God is full of faith (Hebrews 11:1). Likewise, we must be people of faith so as to encourage our children to follow God unwaveringly.

5. God is a provider (Genesis 22:14) - and so must we provide for our family and avoid debts as much as possible. We do not want to leave a legacy of debts.

6. God is obedient even unto the death of the cross (Philippians 2:8); we must be submitted to God and be transparent so that our children will be able to see our obedience to our Heavenly Father.

7. God demonstrated self-control. Likewise, we must demonstrate self-control and become great examples for our children to follow.

8. God provided us security (John 17:12).

9. God showed us love (1 Corinthians 13:3).

Building or rebuilding a family requires us to show these strong pillars of godly character in our lives as parents.

WORDS TO PONDER ON...

"Became all things to all men..."

> *"To the weak became I as weak, that I might gain the weak: I am made all things to all men, that I might by all means save some." (1 Corinthians 9:22)*

When building or rebuilding a family, we must be willing to become all things (as embodiments of godly characteristics) to our family so that we might be able to show God through us to our kids. Charity begins at home; so if we fail at home then we have failed everywhere. You cannot delegate these responsibilities to the school system, the Sunday school or your kids' friends' parent.

ASSIGNMENT

1. What does it mean to have godly character?
2. Which godly character traits are you still lacking or struggling with?
3. Do you teach godly principles to your children?
4. What can your children say about you in one word?

Day 23

GODLY TRAINING

"They which builded on the wall, and they that bare burdens, with those that laded, everyone with one of his hands wrought in the work, and with the other hand held a weapon." (Nehemiah 4:17)

WHY GODLY TRAINING?

Training is the key to everything. When God invented a family system, He also designed an instructional manual to help educate and train so that we can be fulfilled. In any organization, proper employee training is the key to success. Nehemiah's men were trained and seasoned warriors; they worked with one hand and held a weapon in the other. Without proper training, the rebuilding effort would have been greatly hampered.

In the same vein, a family is an organization that requires constant training, and the instruction from the manual is to begin the training while our children are young, and to continue so that they will not depart from the way of the Lord (Proverbs 22:6). The story of Prophet Eli's family is an epic example of a lack of godly training as a result of Eli's failure as a father. The Bible describes the sons of Eli as "sons of Belial" (1 Samuel 2:12-17) —that alone is a label no parent will want on their children, definitely not on a prophet's kids; but unfortunately it was evident in their behavior that they lacked godly training. It is not clearly stated whether they were not trained properly or there was no training at all, but it became obvious that they lacked proper training and manners, especially when dealing with the people of the Lord. They both died a terrible death and one of their wives had a baby named Ichabod which means the glory has departed from Israel—all because a future generation was compromised by lack of godly training.

Noah was a man that feared God greatly; as a result, God revealed to him the future plan of humanity. God asked Noah to build an ark. The difference between the family of Eli and Noah is the evidence of godly training demonstrated by the children of Noah (Genesis 7:7). Noah's children did not ask him "who told you to build what?" They simply complied with God's divine instructions. Even his daughters-in-law respected the integrity of their father and the godly training he must have provided his sons. Godly training is very important and ultimately becomes a difference maker in the lives of the children He has given us. After all, we are the quivers that hold the arrows for Him.

WORDS TO PONDER ON...

"The instructions of the father..."

> *"My son, hear the instruction of thy father, and forsake not the law of thy mother" (Proverbs 1:8)*

It is the responsibility of both father and mother to make sure the instructions from the Lord are taught to their children. The father cannot do it alone; neither can the mother do it alone. My prayer is that the Lord will support all the single parents out there.

ASSIGNMENT

1. Do you know the voice of God?
2. When was the last time you taught your children something?
3. Do you enjoy the company of your children and do they enjoy yours?

Day 24

GODLY DISCIPLINE

"But if ye turn unto me, and keep my commandments, and do them; though there were of you cast out unto the uttermost part of the heaven, yet will I gather them from thence, and will bring them unto the place that I have chosen to set my name there." (Nehemiah 1:9)

WHY GODLY DISCIPLINE?

Nehemiah realized that godly sorrow leads to repentance, so he reminded God of His promise that if the children of Israel sinned, and as a result, the Lord turned against them, it is written that, upon their repentance, God will be merciful and restore them back to their rightful place. No parent wants to needlessly chastise or disengage from their children, but when a child misbehaves, it becomes the duty of a godly parent to discipline and correct.

God's DNA was transferred to us when we received the breath of life and as such we are bound to be disciplined by God when we disobey His words. He does so because of His love for us.

> *"And ye have forgotten the exhortation which speaketh unto you as unto children, My son, despise not thou the chastening of the Lord, nor faint when thou art rebuked of him: For whom the Lord loveth he chasteneth, and scourgeth every son whom he receiveth. If ye endure chastening, God dealeth with you as with sons; for what son is he whom the father chasteneth not? But if ye be without chastisement, whereof all are partakers, then are ye bastards, and not sons." (Hebrews 12:5-8).*

However, God does not tempt us with evil leading to disobedience. Hence, no man can say when he is tempted, I am tempted of God:

> *for God cannot be tempted with evil, neither tempts he any man. (James 1:13-16)*

We are encouraged by James not to err from the right way. There is a need for discipline in a family for such a family to fulfill the will of God and maximize their destiny. Let us consider a few examples in the Bible. When Korah, Datham, Abiram and two hundred and fifty of the princes rose against Moses to question his leadership and God's authority in his life, God's disciplinary action came down swiftly against them; they were swallowed by the earth (Numbers 16).

Another example is that of David when he numbered the children of Israel against God's will; the disciplinary arm of God's love came down on him and the people (1 Chronicle 21). Thank God for the cross of Calvary on which Jesus hung to become our powerful mediator (between us and God); otherwise human race would have been consumed by God.

The Bible encourages us not to withhold correction from our children.

*"Withhold not correction from the child: for if thou beatest him with the rod, he shall not die. Thou shalt beat him with the rod, and shalt deliver his soul from hell." (Proverbs 23:13-14)*The need for godly discipline is in line with God's principle. In reality, the same societal system that complains about you disciplining your child will put him or her in jail as soon as he or she is of age.

Understanding why God disciplines His children will put in perspective why a parent should do the same. God disciplines us out of love. The writer of Hebrews reminds us that "whom the Lord loves He chastened, and scourges every son whom He receives". Likewise, every parent should discipline their children out of love and not out of anger. We lose the purpose of discipline when we allow our anger to take over our emotions. When we are building or rebuilding a family, godly disciple is an important pillar which upholds a family.

WORDS TO PONDER ON...

"No chastening for the present seems to be joyous..."

> *"Now no chastening for the present seemeth to be joyous, but grievous: nevertheless afterward it yieldeth the peaceable fruit of righteousness unto them which are exercised thereby." (Hebrews 12:11)*

No one enjoys discipline—neither kids nor adults—but discipline, when done correctly, yields the peaceable fruit of righteousness unto them which are exercised thereby. Let us endeavor to focus our discipline as parents on obtaining a meaningful corrective measure that will help the child and not damage him or her.

ASSIGNMENT

1. Do you have any relationship with your children?
2. How do you treat your spouse?
3. How do you discipline your children?
4. What outcomes do you anticipate when you discipline?

Day 25

PRAYER AS THE MASTER KEY

"O Lord, I beseech thee, let now thine ear be attentive to the prayer of thy servant, and to the prayer of thy servants, who desire to fear thy name: and prosper, I pray thee, thy servant this day, and grant him mercy in the sight of this man. For I was the king's cupbearer." (Nehemiah 1:11)

WHY PRAY FOR OUR KIDS?

Nehemiah was a praying man! He prayed all manner of prayers—for repentance, for favor with the king and the people, for his adversaries, for unity of the people after the wall was completed, and so on. The Bible encourages us to pray without ceasing because we are not ignorant of the devices of our adversary (1 Thessalonians 5:17; 2 Corinthians 2:11).

In the Gospels, Jesus rebuked His disciples for not allowing parents to bring their children closer to Him.

"Then were there brought unto him little children, that he should put his hands on them, and pray: and the disciples rebuked them. But Jesus said, Suffer little children, and forbid them not, to come unto me: for of such is the kingdom of heaven. And he laid his hands on them, and departed thence." (Matthew 19:13-15)

We can infer from this narration that it is the duty of parents to bring their children to Jesus in prayer, and every time they do so, they are asking Jesus to lay His hand upon them. In the same vein, it is definitely good practice for parents to lay hands on their children while praying for them; I believe that it creates some type of bonding between praying parents and their children. When we are building or rebuilding our family, prayer is another pillar that must be built in order for that family to withstand every wind that might attempt to bring it down.

Why pray for our kids? What are we to pray for? An effective prayer is a prayer that focuses on promises from God's Word. I call them PROMISE-BASED REQUESTS. Let us look at some of such promises from God's Word:

- That our children shall be taught by the Lord, for Jesus to reveal Himself to them and to have the peace of the Lord that comes from knowing Him (Isaiah 53:13).
- That our children shall abide in the word of God, that they may know God through His word (Isaiah 59:21).
- That they will be divinely protected in this era of gross and diverse disasters across the globe (Psalms 108:28).
- That our children shall be filled with the Holy Spirit for divine guidance and leadership (Isaiah 44:3-5).
- That the fear of the Lord which is the beginning of wisdom

will abide in them, so that they guide their affairs with discretion (Psalms 112:1-2).

- That our children will increase in wisdom, stature and favor with God and man (Luke 2:52).
- That they will love to attend church, and choose to make the house of the Lord a place of refuge for their souls (Psalms 27:4).
- That our children will walk in integrity all the days of their lives (Proverbs 20:7).
- That our children will choose good friends and keep away from the companion of fools (Proverbs 13:20)
- And finally, that in all they do, our children will seek first the Kingdom of God and His righteousness (Matthew 6:33).

WORDS TO PONDER ON...

"All prayer and supplication in the Spirit..."

"Praying always with all prayer and supplication in the Spirit, and watching thereunto with all perseverance and supplication for all saints" (Ephesians 6:18)

Paul urged the church in Ephesus to pray always with all kinds of prayer and making supplication in the Spirit. Every parent should ask the Holy Spirit to help them in praying for their children by speaking in tongues, knowing that whoever prays in the spirit speaks mystery and that, my friend, covers everything that is beyond our understanding regarding the lives of our children.

ASSIGNMENT

1. Do you pray for your children?
2. How often do you pray for them?
3. Can your children share their prayer needs with you?
4. Do your children know how to pray for themselves?

Day 26

BUILDING OR REBUILDING A BUSINESS

"And I went out by night by the gate of the valley, even before the dragon well, and to the dung port, and viewed the walls of Jerusalem, which were broken down, and the gates thereof were consumed with fire." (Nehemiah 2:13)

LAYING A GODLY FOUNDATION

Building or rebuilding anything is not an easy task, to say the least - especially when it comes to building or rebuilding a business. In continuation of our gleanings from Nehemiah, our opening text tells us how he went out by night by the gate of the valley, even before the dragon well. What an adventure! To build or rebuild will require us to pull a late night going over ideas and strategies, encountering obstacles and difficulties.

The most important thing about building or rebuilding, however, is how the foundation is laid. 1 Corinthians 3:11 tells us that "For other foundation can no man lay than that is laid, which is Jesus Christ." It all must begin with Jesus, the sure foundation. This is a very important point to make because we know that if the foundation is destroyed, the business owner might not be able to do much (as revealed to us in Psalms 11:3).

So, how do we establish that foundation?

The answer is found in Matthew 7:24-27. Jesus said *"Therefore whosoever heareth these sayings of mine, and doeth them, I will liken him unto a wise man, which built his house upon a rock: And the rain descended, and the floods came, and the winds blew, and beat upon that house; and it fell not: for it was founded upon a rock [Jesus]. And every one that heareth these sayings of mine, and doeth them not, shall be likened unto a foolish man, which built his house upon the sand: And the rain descended, and the floods came, and the winds blew, and beat upon that house; and it fell: and great was the fall of it."*.

In practical terms, building or rebuilding with a good foundation is as simple as hearing and doing the Word of the Lord—and the Bible refers to the Word as Jesus. There's a good story in Luke 5:1-11 that models for us what building or rebuilding our business on Jesus looks like:

> *"And it came to pass, that, as the people pressed upon him to hear the word of God, he stood by the lake of Gennesaret, And saw two ships standing by the lake: but the fishermen were gone out of them, and were washing their nets. And he entered into one of the ships, which was Simon's, and prayed him that he would thrust out a little from the land. And he sat down, and taught the people out of the ship. Now when he had left speaking, he said unto Simon, Launch out into the deep, and let down your nets for a draught. And Simon answering said unto him, Master, we have toiled all the night, and have taken nothing: nevertheless at thy word I will let down the net. And when*

they had this done, they inclosed a great multitude of fishes: and their net brake. And they beckoned unto their partners, which were in the other ship, that they should come and help them. And they came, and filled both the ships, so that they began to sink. When Simon Peter saw it, he fell down at Jesus' knees, saying, Depart from me; for I am a sinful man, O Lord. For he was astonished, and all that were with him, at the draught of the fishes which they had taken: And so was also James, and John, the sons of Zebedee, which were partners with Simon. And Jesus said unto Simon, Fear not; from henceforth thou shalt catch men. And when they had brought their ships to land, they forsook all, and followed him."

To put the story in context, we do not know the relationship between Jesus and Peter as at this time. Peter was just a fisherman who was very frustrated with the way his business went; he and his colleagues had labored all night without any success—a business experience many of us are familiar with, along with its resultant emotions (feelings of frustration and dejection, even to the point of quitting) but as the story unfolds, something unusual happened. Jesus asked Peter if He could use his boat for reaching out to the people that came to hear Him speak. That was the moment the foundation of Peter's business changed forever. Peter obliged and Jesus went ahead with His teaching to the people. We must understand that whether we are building or rebuilding, Jesus must be involved. He's very much interested in our business; He will always ask us if we want Him to come in.

In Luke 5:3, Peter's business partnered with Jesus' ministry which was an outreach tool to the dying world. As we read on, we get to find out that there are many benefits we stand to derive from partnering with Jesus. In Luke 5:4, Jesus instructed Peter to "launch into the deep." When you partner with Jesus, the reward will return to you in multiple folds. Peter was washing his net because the fishing expedition done earlier had failed. Jesus asked him to go back and try again, and the result was awesome! Once your business gets into partnership with Jesus, you too can go back to those old business contacts or opportunities that have failed. Jesus is telling you to go back to them and try those opportunities again.

In verses 5 and 6, Peter followed Jesus' instructions and got a great catch. Likewise, we must allow God's Word to become the lever that moves us, and as we do so, we will always have a bumper harvest. In verse 7, Peter became a blessing to his business associates. In like manner, may your overflowing blessing change the lives of all you do business with in the name of Jesus. In verses 8 and 9, Peter was humbled by the mighty move of God; thus I prophesy into your business that the next round of glory your business shall encounter will humble you and will put your business on the global map. In verse 10, Peter, James and John became instant soul-winners for Jesus, all because they did lend their boat to the Lord. Likewise, I decree that the impact of God's grace on your business will enable you to find reaching out to the lost easier.

We shall consider, in the next few chapters, other exciting discoveries from the Word that will help us build or rebuild our businesses.

WORDS TO PONDER ON...

"Three thousand souls..."

"Then they that gladly received his word were baptized: and the same day there were added unto them about three thousand souls. And they continued stedfastly in the apostles' doctrine and fellowship, and in breaking of bread, and in prayers." (Acts 2:41-42)

Having encountered Jesus and partnered with Him as Peter did in Luke 5, he became the only recorded Apostle that won three thousand souls for Jesus in one altar call. Peter had the opportunity to build a solid foundation with Jesus and he took the opportunity. Let us emulate him for a great catch of souls like this.

ASSIGNMENT

1. Do you know your business can be built on the solid rock?
2. Do you separate yourself from the business?
3. What has your business done for the Kingdom lately?
4. Are you a soul-winner?
5. What other ways can your business partner with the Kingdom?

Day 27

BUILDING INTEGRITY

"Moreover I said unto the king, If it please the king, let letters be given me to the governors beyond the river, that they may convey me over till I come into Judah;" (Nehemiah 2:7)

Nehemiah was a man of impeccable integrity who had served the king for at least twenty years as the cupbearer. Nehemiah had never had a sad countenance before the king. He probably had never 'called in sick' since he started working in the palace; so when he came in with a sad countenance, the king was quick to ask 'why?' He made his request known to the king and it was granted without any reservations—what a man of unquestionable integrity!

Nehemiah asked for a letter for his provision from the king, and the king, knowing who he was, did not ask him much. That speaks volumes! For us to build or rebuild a business, our major focus should be on integrity. The challenge with this is that anytime you over-expose or commit yourself, you stand to lose your integrity rather quickly. The Bible talks about us holding the mystery of the faith in a pure conscience—another way to describe a man or woman of integrity.

How do we become a man or woman of integrity? 1 Timothy 3:1-8 answers the question for us:

> *"This is a true saying, If a man desire the office of a bishop, he desireth a good work. A bishop then must be blameless, the husband of one wife, vigilant, sober, of good behaviour, given to hospitality, apt to teach; Not given to wine, no striker, not greedy of filthy lucre; but patient, not a brawler, not covetous; One that ruleth well his own house, having his children in subjection with all gravity; (For if a man know not how to rule his own house, how shall he take care of the church of God?) Not a novice, lest being lifted up with pride he fall into the condemnation of the devil. Moreover he must have a good report of them which are without; lest he fall into reproach and the snare of the devil. Likewise must the deacons be grave, not doubletongued, not given to much wine, not greedy of filthy lucre; Holding the mystery of the faith in a pure conscience." 1 Timothy 3:1-9*

To read the passage through the eyes of a business person, it will read something like this:

> *This is a true saying, if a man or woman wants to own a business, he or she has a good and great ambition. Such a man or woman must be blameless (be well thought of), must not be sleeping around (what a tragedy the reality is in this regards in the business world today), must be cool, calm and collected (possessing people skills), must be knowledgeable, must not be given to alcohol use, must not be thin-skinned, must not be money hungry, and must have a stable home in order to lead others.*

You might be thinking that the passage speaks to potential bishops and not businessmen, but the synonym of a bishop is an administrator, an overseer or a director. No doubt, these are the qualities of a businessman or woman.

What is the function of integrity? It guides you in all your affairs. "The integrity of the upright shall guide them: but the perverseness of transgressors shall destroy them." (Proverbs 11:3). It protects you from errors. It gives you confidence; you walk securely all day long. It helps you make better decisions, being more careful. It makes you more trustworthy. It gives you more influence, people look up to you. It puts you in control.

How do I develop this quality? Paul the apostle, a man of awesome integrity asked the church to pray for him so that he may live honestly with good conscience. He says, "Pray for us: for we trust we have a good conscience, in all things willing to live honestly." (Hebrews 13:18)

It requires a prayerful life to be a man or woman of integrity. It requires a constant look at the perfect law of liberty which is the Word of God. It requires living a self-controlled and selfless lifestyle.

> *"Providing for honest things, not only in the sight of the Lord, but also in the sight of men." (2 Corinthians 8:21)*

WORDS TO PONDER ON...

"Getting riches not by right..."

> *"The heart is deceitful above all things, and desperately wicked: who can know it? I the Lord search the heart, I try the reins, even to give every man according to his ways, and according to the fruit of his doings. As*

the partridge sitteth on eggs, and hatcheth them not; so he that getteth riches, and not by right, shall leave them in the midst of his days, and at his end shall be a fool." (Jeremiah 17:9-11)

Integrity is a matter of the heart and a function of a pure conscience. The Bible likens a lack of integrity to a partridge that sits on eggs and "hatcheth them not; so he that getteth riches, and not by right, shall leave them in the midst of his days." Lack of integrity is a poison.

ASSIGNMENT

1. What is integrity to you?
2. What are the qualities of a person of integrity?
3. What was your last act that shows your integrity?
4. If not, when will you do something that speaks volume about your integrity?

Day 28

DEVELOPING KNOWLEDGE OF WITTY INVENTIONS AND WISE PLANNING

"Then the king said unto me, For what dost thou make request? So I prayed to the God of heaven. And I said unto the king, If it please the king, and if thy servant have found favour in thy sight, that thou wouldest send me unto Judah, unto the city of my fathers' sepulchres, that I may build it. And the king said unto me, (the queen also sitting by him,) For how long shall thy journey be? and when wilt thou return? So it pleased the king to send me; and I set him a time." (Nehemiah 2:4-6)

It was recorded that it took Nehemiah about six months before he acted on the information given to him by Hanani, from the month of Chisleu to the month of Nisan. It requires a great deal of wise planning and a God-given idea to build or rebuild anything. The king asked Nehemiah, "What is your request?" Imagine Nehemiah saying "Sir, let me think about it for a week and I will get back to you" – not only would he have had his request denied, but it might have even cost him his life because he was not allowed to have a sad countenance as a cupbearer.

Developing wittiness and wise planning is not only required to build or rebuild, but lacking it could simply mean that your business idea is dead on arrival. A God-given idea is far better than a thousand good ideas and wise planning is very much needed for a God-given idea to materialize.

Let us look at the Bible for directions. Proverbs 8:12 shows us where the knowledge of witty inventions comes from: it comes from the wisdom of the Lord! "I wisdom dwell with prudence, and find out knowledge of witty inventions." Divine idea is what sets us apart from other businesses operated by unbelievers. A good example of this is well illustrated in Genesis 30:31-43:

> *"And he said, What shall I give thee? And Jacob said, Thou shalt not give me any thing: if thou wilt do this thing for me, I will again feed and keep thy flock: I will pass through all thy flock to day, removing from thence all the speckled and spotted cattle, and all the brown cattle among the sheep, and the spotted and speckled among the goats: and of such shall be my hire. So shall my righteousness answer for me in time to come, when it shall come for my hire before thy face: every one that is not speckled and spotted among the goats, and brown among the sheep, that shall be counted stolen with me. And Laban said, Behold, I would it might be according to thy word. And he removed that day the he goats that were ringstraked and spotted, and all the she goats that were speckled and spotted, and every one that had some white in it, and all the brown among the sheep, and gave them into the hand of his sons. And he set three days' journey betwixt himself and Jacob: and Jacob fed the rest of Laban's flocks.*
>
> *And Jacob took him rods of green poplar, and of the hazel and chesnut tree; and pilled white strakes in them, and made the white appear*

which was in the rods. And he set the rods which he had pilled before the flocks in the gutters in the watering troughs when the flocks came to drink, that they should conceive when they came to drink. And the flocks conceived before the rods, and brought forth cattle ringstraked, speckled, and spotted. And Jacob did separate the lambs, and set the faces of the flocks toward the ringstraked, and all the brown in the flock of Laban; and he put his own flocks by themselves, and put them not unto Laban's cattle. And it came to pass, whensoever the stronger cattle did conceive, that Jacob laid the rods before the eyes of the cattle in the gutters, that they might conceive among the rods. But when the cattle were feeble, he put them not in: so the feebler were Laban's, and the stronger Jacob's. And the man increased exceedingly, and had much cattle, and maidservants, and menservants, and camels, and asses."

Jacob had been working for Laban for a while without anything to show for it, so he approached Laban that he would like to start his own cattle rearing business. Laban and Jacob struck a deal on what should be his payment for his services and the agreement was quickly reached. In signing off on this deal, Jacob made an interesting statement. He said "let my righteousness answer for me in time to come." What a statement! Jacob was basically saying to Laban, "my integrity will stand up to you in the time of doubt about the outcome of our business dealings."

In any case, Jacob got an idea to advance his cattle rearing endeavors and the result will amaze anyone. What did Jacob do? Jacob, upon receiving a divine idea and guidance—which is available to all of us if we care enough to ask Him—took a simple rod and did the unimaginable with it. The result in verse 43 says "And the man increased exceedingly, and had much cattle…"

My mentor and father in the Lord, Bishop David Oyedepo once said something intriguing. When someone asked him a question about how the church was able to do so much in such a given time, his answer was quite simple but profound: "We don't do any project unless it is commanded!" Simple, but profound. No wonder he's such a trailblazer and innovator.

Where did Jacob learn to do this — to tap into divine ideas? I am sure he learnt from his father. Isaac invented irrigation farming in his day to the point that the Philistine envied him and his God-given idea became a threat to them.

At this juncture, you may want to ask; how can someone get access to God-given ideas? The answer is the Holy Ghost! He's the custodian of everything divine.

> *"But the Comforter, which is the Holy Ghost, whom the Father will send in my name, he shall teach you all things, and bring all things to your remembrance, whatsoever I have said unto you." (John 14:26)*

This is why it is a must that every Christian business man or woman be filled with Holy Spirit with the evidence of speaking in tongues. When building or rebuilding, you must engage the Holy Spirit. There's a great need for wise planning for the revelation of the Spirit to develop into a meaningful enterprise.

In this regard, King Solomon, the wise man, gave a piece of advice in Proverbs 24:3-4:

> *"Through wisdom is an house builded; and by understanding it is established: And by knowledge shall the chambers be filled with all precious and pleasant riches."*

The Living Bible puts it even more clearly:

> *"Any enterprise is built or rebuilt by wise planning, becomes strong through common sense and profits wonderfully by keeping abreast of the facts."*

How to keep abreast of the facts will be discussed further in the next few chapters.

WORDS TO PONDER ON...

"The secret things..."

> *"The secret things belong unto the Lord our God: but those things which are revealed belong unto us and to our children forever, that we may do all the words of this law." (Deuteronomy 29:29).*

God has a lot of things that He wants to reveal to us so that we can build or rebuild successfully. As you may know, this is an exclusive preserve of those who choose to dwell in the secret place of the Most High—those who have access to secret things in a secret place—all found in Jesus Christ by the help of the Holy Spirit.

ASSIGNMENT

1. What is the level of your relationship with the Holy Spirit?
2. How do you know when an idea is God-given?
3. What are your decision-making strategies?
4. Have you ever experienced any God-given idea?

Day 29

TREATING PEOPLE RIGHT

"Then said I unto them, Ye see the distress that we are in, how Jerusalem lieth waste, and the gates thereof are burned with fire: come, and let us build up the wall of Jerusalem, that we be no more a reproach. Then I told them of the hand of my God which was good upon me; as also the king's words that he had spoken unto me. And they said, Let us rise up and build. So they strengthened their hands for this good work." (Nehemiah 2:17-18)

TREATING YOUR WORKERS AND CUSTOMERS RIGHT

Nehemiah was living in the palace with the king; as such, his daily portions were well supplied. He probably wore fine clothing, since, as a cupbearer, he was one of the king's most trusted aides. Everything was going well for him--which honestly suggests that the care of the people back in Jerusalem should be less of his concern--but not this guy. He wanted to be treated like his people, which explains why he later became the governor of his people. He treated his people with respect.

Drawing applicable principles to the business world from this, one of the core values of any business should be adding value to people - both to the workers and the customers. Proverbs 3:27-28 lays the foundation upon which all relationships, especially with the employees and the customers must be laid: *"Withhold not good from them to whom it is due, when it is in the power of thine hand to do it. Say not unto thy neighbour,Go, and come again, and to morrow I will give; when thou hast it by thee."*

I will give you my own example here. I had been in a business for a while and there came a time when the business was struggling to meet its obligations, especially with regard to paying our employees on time. I decided not to pay myself until all the employees were fully paid. In fact, to some, I paid interest on their salaries; to others, I reimbursed their late payment on their car or rent; and to some others still, I paid the insufficient fund fees accrued from my bounced check. Finally, when the situation did not change l decided to close about two or three offices. I went into debt because of that situation! In retrospect, that was a bad decision and I encourage anyone not to go into debt.

The rationale for sharing this personal story is to illustrate that you must not withhold anything--especially the salaries of your employees. When your employees are not happy then your customers will never be happy with your services.

Let us look at two examples from the Bible. Again the story of Laban and Jacob illustrates how bad a workplace relationship can be. The story started in Genesis 28 when Isaac sent his son to live with Laban, his uncle. Jacob became one of his employees and a deal was struck: wages for his labor. They agreed to the first seven years after which Rachel was supposed to be given to Jacob but Laban withheld that good from him. Jacob became furious but signed another contract for another seven years. Finally, he got Rachel as initially agreed. In the process, Laban changed Jacob's wages seven times and treated him very badly, but God was paying attention. Fast forward to Genesis 31, Laban had gone bankrupt while Jacob prospered exceedingly.

> *"And he heard the words of Laban's sons, saying, Jacob hath taken away all that was our father's; and of that which was our father's hath he gotten all this glory. And Jacob beheld the countenance of Laban, and, behold, it was not toward him as before. And the Lord said unto Jacob, Return unto the land of thy fathers, and to thy kindred; and I will be with thee." (Genesis 31:1-3)*

The other example is the story of King David who was supposed to be at war but decided to stay back in his palace. He went upon the roof and saw Bathsheba. He committed adultery with her and later killed her husband all because he violated employee-employer relationship. (2 Samuel 11). When building or rebuilding your business, treating your employees and customers right is a sure recipe for success.

WORDS TO PONDER ON...

"As you would that men should do to you..."

> *"And as ye would that men should do to you, do ye also to them likewise." (Luke 6:31)*

This should be the gold standard statement in any business core value. Every time you are about to do something to your employees or customers, put yourself in their shoes.

ASSIGNMENT

1. What are your people skills?
2. What benefits do you provide for your employees?
3. Are your employees paid well and on time?
4. What would you do differently from now on?

Day 30

FAITHFULNESS IN FINANCIAL MATTERS WITH GOD

"And a letter unto Asaph the keeper of the king's forest, that he may give me timber to make beams for the gates of the palace which appertained to the house, and for the wall of the city, and for the house that I shall enter into. And the king granted me, according to the good hand of my God upon me. Then I came to the governors beyond the river, and gave them the king's letters. Now the king had sent captains of the army and horsemen with me." (Nehemiah 2:8-9)

Nehemiah was a faithful servant to the king; he was well liked. While there was nothing recorded in the Bible about their financial dealing, it remains evident that he was a reliable and trusted aide. The king trusted his own life to Nehemiah because the cupbearer to a king occupied a position through which the king could be easily poisoned. God is looking for such faithful ambassadors like Nehemiah today, especially in the area of financial matters.

Let us establish some facts quickly: The earth is the Lord's and the fullness thereof! By implication, God does not need us for His needs to be met. As a matter of fact, God has no needs in that sense. He owns the cattle upon a thousand hills! If God were to be hungry, none of us would be qualified to feed Him. God owns all the gold and silver thereof here on earth and everywhere else.

Now that we have established these premises, then you will understand that your financial faithfulness is for your benefit, not God's! It has been said many times over that if you want to know who loves God and assess their faithfulness, all you need to check is their checkbook. When you are building or rebuilding a business, it is very important at the beginning to establish God as a strategic and financial partner. It is also important to establish this relationship at a personal level. Proverbs 3:9-10 instructs us to honor the Lord with our substance.

> *"Honour the Lord with thy substance, and with the firstfruits of all thine increase: So shall thy barns be filled with plenty, and thy presses shall burst out with new wine." (Proverbs 3:9-10)*

When we honor the Lord with our substance, things go well with us and with our business. And we should understand that our substance is definitely referring to much more than money. When you honor the Lord with your substance, the reward is that your barn will be filled with plenty—and that's prosperity, my friend.

I have been able to identify six things that I consider as our substance with which we can honor God as we build or rebuild. They include: 1) Tongue 2) Time 3) Talent 4) Treasure 5) Transportation. 6). Turf

HONORING THE LORD WITH YOUR SUBSTANCE

1. Tongue

Your tongue is the greatest weapon and a substance that can bring great increase to you. James 3 tells us that where your tongue goes is where your whole body is going. If you love life and want to see good days, scriptures advise us to keep our tongue from speaking guile. When your word honors God, it will bring wholeness and wealth to your life.

2. Time

When you spend your time well in doing things that advance the Kingdom agenda, then you are honoring God. Time is money; when you spend time in God's presence, you get paid big and that's prosperity. I once said that whoever wastes your time is a silent killer. Jesus said I must work the works of him that sent me while it is day. That is effective time management! And guess what? It will bring tremendous amount of benefits to one's life.

3. Talent

Your gifts, whatever they are—your ability to sing, play sport, play an instrument, whatever your gifting is—must honor God; and when that happens, it leads to automatic lifting.

4. Treasure

The Bible talks about putting your treasure where moths cannot destroy it. When your money does not honor God, that means you are putting it in places where it will be devoured. Giving your tithe and offering is the surest way to divine lifting. God opens the windows of heaven on your behalf. Picture that in your mind because the thought of it alone should be music to any ear.

5. Transportation

Your vehicle is one of the most important items amongst your substance with which you can honor God if you allow God to use it. When Jesus was going to Jerusalem He asked to use someone else's colt. What a glorious entrance to the city of Jerusalem! I can only imagine the amount of material blessings the man got. So, ask yourself, when was the last time you gave anyone a ride (to church or elsewhere)? When last did you help somebody with your vehicle? Those are questions for you to answer.

6. Turf

This refers to your house. When Jesus sent out His disciples two by two, He told them to abide in any house that would accommodate them, and that if they were accommodated, the peace of God in their lives would abide upon that house. You need more of the peace of God? Then open your house up for God to use it!

The Bible also commands us to bring our tithes and offering to the house of God.

> *"Bring ye all the tithes into the storehouse, that there may be meat in mine house, and prove me now herewith, saith the Lord of hosts, if I will not open you the windows of heaven, and pour you out a blessing, that there shall not be room enough to receive it. And I will rebuke the devourer for your sakes, and he shall not destroy the fruits of your ground; neither shall your vine cast her fruit before the time in the field, saith the Lord of hosts. And all nations shall call you blessed: for ye shall be a delightsome land, saith the Lord of hosts." (Malachi 3:10-12)*

Note that God's command is that we bring all of our tithes—not some—and all the time. So, whether you are building or rebuilding your business, there must be a personal and business commitment in the area of bringing your tithe and offering. The result of obedience is clearly stated for us to see in your life and business. It opens the windows of heaven, and pours you a blessing—the blessing is poured out, not that it drips—and there will not be enough room to receive it. The God of heaven promises to see to it that the devourer is rebuked for your sake. The fruits of your ground and your vine are preserved. Believe it, because this is what the Lord is saying to you as a result of your obedience. All the nations shall call you blessed. Everybody will want to do business with you and customers will prefer your business to your competitors.

The principle of tithing from one's business was first shared to my knowledge by my mentor and father in the Lord, Bishop David Oyedepo. Let us take a beautiful journey together to the book of Genesis 14:14-20 where Abraham, our patriarch of faith, gave the tithe of all—personally and corporately—to Melchizedek.

> *"And when Abram heard that his brother was taken captive, he armed his trained servants, born in his own house, three hundred and eighteen, and pursued them unto Dan. And he divided himself against them, he and his servants, by night, and smote them, and pursued them unto Hobah, which is on the left hand of Damascus. And he brought back all the goods, and also brought again his brother Lot, and his goods, and the women also, and the people. And the king of Sodom went out to meet him after his return from the slaughter of Chedorlaomer, and of the kings that were with him, at the valley of Shaveh, which is the king's dale. And Melchizedek king of Salem brought forth bread and wine: and he was the priest of the most high God. And he blessed him, and said, Blessed be Abram of the most high God, possessor*

of heaven and earth: And blessed be the most high God, which hath delivered thine enemies into thy hand. And he gave him tithes of all." (Genesis 14:14-20)

Observe that the tithes given in the passage were not the result of personal income to Abraham but as a result of the spoil from war corporately produced by his warriors. The story provides a backdrop to us for the reason behind Abraham's greatness and wealth. It is very important, whether you are building or rebuilding your business, to tithe from it. (A tithe represents the tenth of your profit from the business.) Tithing corporately takes your stewardship and the result to another level of fruitfulness.

WORDS TO PONDER ON...

"Will a man rob God?"

"Will a man rob God? Yet ye have robbed me. But ye say, Wherein have we robbed thee? In tithes and offerings." (Malachi 3:8)

When a man or woman does not pay his or her tithe, it amounts to robbing God. And the Bible is very clear on what to do when a thief is caught in the act: He or she must restore back seven folds.

"Men do not despise a thief, if he steal to satisfy his soul when he is hungry; But if he be found, he shall restore sevenfold; he shall give all the substance of his house." (Proverbs 6:30-31)

I know we are no longer under the law, but we must not forget that Abraham tithed before the law was given. Your tithing has nothing to do with the Old or New Testaments; it is purely a God-thing. Obedience is better than sacrifice.

ASSIGNMENT

1. What has your business done for God lately?
2. Have you ever heard about the principle of tithing and offering?
3. Have you ever given tithe and offering?
4. What is tithe in percentage?
5. What is offering? What does it represent?

Day 31

THE POWER OF CONTINUOUS TRAINING AND IMPROVEMENT

"In what place therefore ye hear the sound of the trumpet, resort ye thither unto us: our God shall fight for us. So we laboured in the work: and half of them held the spears from the rising of the morning till the stars appeared." (Nehemiah 4:20-21)

The power of continuous training and improvement, especially in the area of personal development, cannot be overemphasized. Every process requires a constant evaluation in order to be adjusted as needed for any enterprise to be able to continue to yield value. Nehemiah was obviously a man that believed in process, as it became quite obvious in his training style and technique. There were clear instructions on hand on how to respond when the people heard the sound of the trumpet, where to gather, and what to do there. From our opening verse we can see him address the how, when, where and what, which are the essential elements of a good training and improvement protocol.

For any enterprise to thrive, there are three elements that must be carefully considered: wise planning, use of common sense and keeping abreast of the facts (continuous training and improvement) as stated in Proverbs 24:3-4:

> *"Any enterprise is built by wise planning, becomes strong through common sense, and profits wonderfully by keeping abreast of the facts." (Living Bible)*

Let us consider two instances from the scriptures. Peter was one of Jesus' first disciples and his right-hand man. For three and a half years, they were together. Peter was a fisherman by trade—which, by the way, tells us that it is possible for anybody to fulfill the plan of God for his or her life without a college degree—but he had a lot of rough edges that needed smoothening. It is documented many times in the Bible that, after Jesus had departed physically, Peter was more particular about the salvation of the Jews; he did not make a priority of improving his understanding of the New Covenant and its benefits. As the story unfolds, the Bible tells us of how an angel of the Lord appeared to Peter and instructed him to go to Cornelius. He hesitated before obeying that instruction, perhaps because he did not desire to expand his knowledge of the New Testament and the universality of the availability of grace. Acts 4:13 reveals that though Peter and John were bold in their convictions, they appeared to be unlearned and ignorant. I personally believe that Peter could have done more in the Kingdom if he had developed his knowledge about the extension of grace to the Gentiles.

On the other hand is Paul who, from his conversion in Acts 9, became a man on a mission, ready to defend what he believed at any cost. The Bible records that while on his way to Damascus, he had all the necessary authority to inflict a lot of harm to the body of Christ. Jesus saw something interesting about Paul, and

He revealed to Ananias why He chose Paul for His assignment.

> *"But the Lord said unto him, Go thy way: for he is a chosen vessel unto me, to bear my name before the Gentiles, and kings, and the children of Israel: For I will shew him how great things he must suffer for my name's sake." (Acts 9:15-16)*

I believe that Jesus saw his zeal for knowledge and his potential to be the man to get the attention of the scholars of that time. He was to present Jesus before the Gentiles, kings and the highly skilled children of Israel.

It is quite evident that Paul was very studious, as he wrote two-thirds of the entire New Testament. Acts 26:24-26 particularly shows that Festus was so upset and impressed about the level of knowledge of Paul that he told him that much learning was affecting his sanity.

> *"And as he thus spake for himself, Festus said with a loud voice, Paul, thou art beside thyself; much learning doth make thee mad. But he said, I am not mad, most noble Festus; but speak forth the words of truth and soberness. For the king knoweth of these things, before whom also I speak freely: for I am persuaded that none of these things are hidden from him; for this thing was not done in a corner."*

Paul read quite often, whether alone, in prison or on the mission field. At a time, he gave an instructive instruction to Timothy:

"The cloak that I left at Troas with Carpus, when thou comest, bring with thee, and the books, but especially the parchments." (2 Timothy 4:13)

Obviously, Paul was always learning and, as such, he was able to reach many more people than all the apostles that actually spent time with Jesus. Paul even admitted that he was the least of the apostles but did more than them all. Why? He was an avid reader and learner.

> *"But by the grace of God I am what I am: and his grace which was bestowed upon me was not in vain; but I laboured more abundantly than they all: yet not I, but the grace of God which was with me." (1 Corinthians 15:10)*

Daniel, Hananiah, Mishael and Azariah were men of substance and self-worth, who took the time to develop their knowledge and as such became men of influence in the old Babylon and represented God well among the pagan nation.

> *"Children in whom was no blemish, but well favoured, and skilful in all wisdom, and cunning in knowledge, and understanding science, and such as had ability in them to stand in the king's palace, and whom they might teach the learning and the tongue of the Chaldeans. And the king communed with them; and among them all was found none like Daniel, Hananiah, Mishael, and Azariah: therefore stood they before the king. And in all matters of wisdom and understanding, that the king enquired of them, he found them ten times better than all the magicians and astrologers that were in all his realm." (Daniel 1:4, 19-20)*

Daniel, in particular, said of himself:

> *"In the first year of his reign I Daniel understood by books the number of the years, whereof the word of the Lord came to Jeremiah the prophet, that he would accomplish seventy years in the desolations of Jerusalem. And I set my face unto the Lord God, to seek by prayer and supplications, with fasting, and sackcloth, and ashes." (Daniel 9:2-3)*

Building or rebuilding a business will require dedication and most importantly the need to constantly re-evaluate and make necessary improvement. Self-development is a must! This involves attending seminars, trade shows and even enrolling in a degree program or some certificate course in order to improve your chances and influence in your space.

WORDS TO PONDER ON...

"My people are destroyed…"

> *"My people are destroyed for lack of knowledge: because thou hast rejected knowledge, I will also reject thee, that thou shalt be no priest to me: seeing thou hast forgotten the law of thy God, I will also forget thy children." (Hosea 4:6)*

God revealed that the simplest thing destroying His people is a lack of knowledge. Every time we do not improve or refuse to increase our knowledge, we are simply rejecting promotion. There's no shortcut to developing our abilities to the fullest. It is for our benefit that we must do it.

ASSIGNMENT

1. How much knowledge do you have operating your business?
2. What is your level of education?
3. When was the last time you attended a seminar?
4. Do you have an appraisal system in place?
5. Do you have a mentor?

Day 32

THE BONDAGE BREAKER

"And our adversaries said, They shall not know, neither see, till we come in the midst among them, and slay them, and cause the work to cease." (Nehemiah 4:11)

OVERCOMING ADDICTIONS

Nehemiah had some strong and defiant adversaries, and they stood to test and destroy the wall. They basically did not want progress of any sort. Nehemiah did not have a known addiction—at least, none was ever documented in the Bible. However, like Nehemiah's adversaries, addiction can be an enemy that has only one purpose which is to destroy its host. Nehemiah's adversaries said, "They shall not know, neither see till we come in the midst among them, and slay them, and cause the work to cease."

This sounds like the modus operandi of addiction—be it to alcohol, sex, pornography, gambling, shopping, overeating, not eating enough, drugs and anything than can be abused. An addiction usually creeps in stealthily. We often don't pay much attention to it until it becomes a serious problem that cannot be controlled any longer. What addiction does is to cause our lives to freeze and become very dysfunctional. Often, it causes pain beyond repair which eventually leads to losses in multiple areas of life.

The good news, however, is that God is able to deliver anyone from any form of addiction. The Bible tells us that everything that God created was good (Genesis 1:31), and it is still good. In Matthew 19:8, when the people were asking Jesus whether it was alright to divorce, His answer was simple and profound; He said "in the beginning, it was not so." Jesus was basically telling the people that most of the problems we encounter are man-made, because from the beginning it was not so. God created humanity so He could have fellowship with us. God came down in the cool of the day to have fellowship with Adam and Eve until Satan entered the scene.

Let us look at a few examples in the Bible how the devil was and still is the influencer and encourager of these terrible problems. In Genesis 3, Satan deceived Eve and changed the course of events in the human race forever.

> *"Now the serpent was more subtil than any beast of the field which the Lord God had made. And he said unto the woman, Yea, hath God said, Ye shall not eat of every tree of the garden? And the woman said unto the serpent, We may eat of the fruit of the trees of the garden: But of the fruit of the tree which is in the midst of the garden, God hath said, Ye shall not eat of it, neither shall ye touch it, lest ye die. And the serpent said unto the woman, Ye shall not surely die" (1-3).*

Another example is in Job 1:6. According to the writer of the book of Job, there was a day when the sons of God came to present themselves before the Lord, and Satan also came among them. From that point on, the life of Job turned upside down. In Mark 4:15, Jesus told His disciples the parable of the sower in which, as He interpreted, the sower sowed the word and Satan came immediately to take away the word from some of the recipients. *"And these are they by the way side, where the word is sown; but when they have heard, Satan cometh immediately, and taketh away the word that was sown in their hearts." (Mark 4:15)* Finally, there is the story of Judas in Luke 22:3. The Bible tells us that Satan entered into him and the result was that he betrayed Jesus and committed suicide.

What do all of these stories have in common? Satan! Addictions happen when we allow the devil to come into our lives. There are many people who refer to their addiction as demons. I am not writing to tell you that I have the cure for any addiction nor am I an expert, but one thing I know is that, in these stories, Satan was able to come in when the victims were away from God. Jesus is the chain-breaker; He came so as to destroy the works of the devil (1 John 3:8). And most certainly, it is never too late to start rebuilding your life again! Remember, dry bones shall live again (Ezekiel 37).

There are five things that I have seen or studied that can prevent us or help us break any form of addiction if we choose to do what is right for us and our families. These include: Socialization, Association, Time Taking, Accountability and Neglect.

How we socialize can be the beginning of our addiction; and who we associate with has everything to do with this. Where and how we spend our time might be another avenue through which we can stop the terrible demon called addiction. Who are you accountable to? If there is no form of accountability in one's life, one becomes a prime candidate for addiction. What are you neglecting? What is taking your attention? Anything that can cheaply steal your attention might be a sign of a potential problem of addiction. See you in the next few chapters as we explore this further.

WORDS TO PONDER ON...

"While men slept..."

> *"But while men slept, his enemy came and sowed tares among the wheat, and went his way." (Matthew 13:25)*

This statement which was spoken by Jesus could as well mean "while we were not paying attention, the enemy came and sowed tears into our lives and went his way." Addiction can be a life-long struggle if we refuse to first recognize the source of the problem and design an appropriate action plan to tackle it. Jesus is the same yesterday, today, and forever; He's still in the business of destroying the yokes of Satan. It doesn't matter how long or how many.

ASSIGNMENT

1. Where do you socialize?
2. Who do you associate with?
3. How do you manage your time?
4. Who are you accountable to?
5. What is stealing your attention?

Day 33

THE EFFECT OF SOCIALIZATION

"The words of Nehemiah the son of Hachaliah. And it came to pass in the month Chisleu, in the twentieth year, as I was in Shushan the palace" (Nehemiah 1:1)

What does it mean to socialize? According to the dictionary, it simply means to make social—to make fit for life in companionship with others. Socialization is a continuous process whereby an individual acquires a personal identity and learns the norms, values, behaviors and social skills appropriate to his or her social position. Nehemiah was a man who had lived in captivity for at least twenty years, based on the date the report of the condition of the wall of Jerusalem was given to him. He lived in the palace and had both influence and affluence. Being the king's cupbearer says a lot about him in that kingdom, but he refused to acquire the identity and learn the norms, values and behaviors of the Persian people who were idolaters.

Addiction to anything begins when we choose to acquire a personal identity and learn the norms, values, behaviors and social skills that are completely contrary to the word of God. As earlier pointed out, addiction creeps in unawares, presents itself as something that you could stop whenever you feel like—until you can't. Unfortunately, it can grow on our watch to become a monster that refuses to be tamed and eventually stops us from moving forward with our lives. Addiction through socialization makes the impact of the Word disappear so quickly because of the continuous process of acquiring personalities that do not conform to the image of Christ.

There are four things that I have identified in the study of people who have been exposed to any addiction due to the influence of socialization; they are: lack of sensitivity, lack of security in their own personality, lack of sincerity, and lack of soundness—not allowing common sense to prevail.

LACK OF SENSITIVITY

Addiction is an adversarial enemy that aims to destroy its host. Nehemiah was concerned about the situation in Jerusalem and came with the permission from the king to repair the wall that was broken down; what a noble cause! Even though he did not reside in Jerusalem, he was still willing to risk his life to appear before the king with a sad countenance. And while you will expect such a selfless person to be received and applauded by his people, it was the contrary that happened. There were adversaries willing to stop his progress. The good thing is that Nehemiah was able to identify the opposition in time because he was very sensitive to his environment and by the help of the Spirit of God.

Every time we let our guard down and lose our sensitivity, we become vulnerable to attack. Addiction does not develop in one night but the seed is sown in one night and it grows as long as we are not sensitive to its influence. The Holy Spirit is our Helper—if and when we depend on Him. He guides us away from every negative influence.

We should endeavor to be sensitive to our environment and the people around us. Self-control and awareness is a must for anyone who wants to escape any form of addiction. The Bible encourages us not to be conformed to this world, but to be transformed away from the norms, values and behavior of anyone who wants to steer us away from God. Our sensitivity increases by renewing our mind with the Word by which we are able to prove what is the good, acceptable and perfect, will of God for our lives.

> *"And be not conformed to this world: but be ye transformed by the renewing of your mind, that ye may prove what is that good, and acceptable, and perfect, will of God." (Romans 12:2)*

LACK OF SECURITY IN PERSONALITY

Addiction becomes a major problem in people who are not secured in who they are. The need to please others has led many down the path of addiction. Nehemiah was a sensitive man who quickly identified his adversaries and dealt with them accordingly. How did he deal with them? He understood very well his position with God. He was highly secured in who he was; therefore he was not easily intimidated by his adversaries.

Addiction is an unassuming adversary that will take over our lives when we lose our identity to its crisis and lose sight of our position in Christ. By the virtue of our position in Christ, adversaries should not even come near us, because the Bible reveals to us that we are seated with Christ in the heavenly places. It is very important for us to know who we are and accept who we are; this might be the beginning of our freedom from addiction.

Who are we? We are created in the image of God, so there's no need to be comparing yourself to anyone else (Genesis 1:27). God knows us before we were even conceived in the belly and separated us to be unique. "Before I formed thee in the belly I knew thee; and before thou camest forth out of the womb I sanctified thee, and I ordained thee a prophet unto the nations." (Jeremiah 1:5)

We are fearfully and wonderfully made! (Psalm 139:14) We are a masterpiece and an ornament of the grace of God. Be sure of yourself and always have the sense of self-worth, knowing that with God on your side, you become a person of influence.

LACK OF SINCERITY

Addiction is a subtle enemy and merely denying its existence might be the path that leads to a place where recovery becomes almost impossible. Nehemiah was not only sensitive to his adversaries, he was very secured in his relationship with God and could not be intimidated. He was sincere with himself and never overestimated or underestimated the wiles of the adversary. Knowing your enemy gives you an advantage in defeating them. A problem known, as they say, is half solved.

An addiction is a problem and not a sin but what led to the addiction might be the source of sin. The Bible tells us that whosoever covers his or her problem (knowing that they have the problem) shall not prosper which simply means in a plain language that such an individual will not get any help. The later part of that scripture reveals what will happen to someone who is very sincere. Such an individual will receive mercy or help. "*He that covereth his sins shall not prosper: but whoso confesseth and forsaketh them shall have mercy." (Proverbs 28:13)*

Being sincere is the beginning of the cure, but if you continue to be addicted, you will reap that reward. God is not mocked and you are not mocked either, because you both know the truth that as long as you continue to deny the truth and not being fully sincere, you will end up in a total disaster (Galatians 6:7). It is your responsibility to do yourself some good. The Bible tells us that to him or her that knows how to do good and refuses to do it, it becomes a sin (James 4:17). Like I wrote earlier, an addiction is a problem and not a sin, but ignoring it is a big sin—because you are willfully destroying the temple of God which is YOU.

LACK OF SOUNDNESS

Common sense appears not be common these days. People literally walk into trouble with their eyes wide open. Nehemiah was a very wise man and was able to deliver himself from a lot of trouble, especially when his adversaries invited him to come to the valley of Ono so that they could talk. He was able to turn down the invitation knowing that it was a trap set up to kill him.

Addiction is a trap set up by the adversary to catch whosoever is void of understanding or common sense. Many times, the use of common sense is all it takes to say no to a friend whom you know has a drug addiction problem inviting you to hang out together. The Bible tells us that when a man refuses to use common sense, such a man shall remain in the congregation of the dead. "The man that wandereth out of the way of understanding shall remain in the congregation of the dead." (Proverbs 21:16)

The use of common sense will keep you from evil every day.

When you engage your common sense, it will prevent your life from unnecessary turmoil.

> *"If thou be wise, thou shalt be wise for thyself: but if thou scornest, thou alone shalt bear it." (Proverbs 9:12)*

Nehemiah was not only sensitive, he was secured, sincere and sound by applying common sense. As a result, he was able to finish the wall in fifty-two days. And as you are the Nehemiah of your generation, guide yourself accordingly.

> *"In the lips of him that hath understanding wisdom is found: but a rod is for the back of him that is void of understanding." (Proverbs 10:13)*

WORDS TO PONDER ON...

"For that which I do I allow not..."

> *"For that which I do I allow not: for what I would, that do I not; but what I hate, that do I. If then I do that which I would not, I consent unto the law that it is good. Now then it is no more I that do it, but sin that dwelleth in me." (Romans 7:15-17).*

When you socialize without establishing your boundaries, you might end up with an addiction. Paul shows how dominating an addiction can be to any life. In his description, he said that the thing he wanted to do, he could not do, but what he did not desire to do took over his life. This simply summarizes the power an addiction can have over any individual. Do well to socialize with caution.

ASSIGNMENT

1. Are you a sensitive person?

2. Are you secured in your personality?

3. Are you sincere with yourself?

4. Are you applying common sense daily?

Day 34

THE PROBLEM WITH BAD COMPANY

"But when Sanballat the Horonite, and Tobiah the servant, the Ammonite, and Geshem the Arabian, heard it, they laughed us to scorn, and despised us, and said, What is this thing that ye do? will ye rebel against the king?" (Nehemiah 2:19)

Sanballat, Tobiah and Geshem are names synonymous with evil—what a terrible company for anyone to be associated with! Anytime you avoid bad company, you avoid a problem. Nehemiah quickly identified these horrible men who had invited him many times to come and associate with them, and their intention was to stop the progress of the work but he denied their invitation every time. Addiction sometimes creeps into one's life through wrong association.

Who are your associates? "Can two walk together, except they be agreed?" (Amos 3:3)To associate is to connect or bring into relation. I have seen many lives destroyed because of association.

If someone you love starts to behave strangely, pay close attention to his or her company. It has been said again and again, "show me your friend, and I will tell you who you are." As habits are learned, so also are addictions. If you stay around the wrong company long enough, you will attract their addiction. There are three things that I have seen in life that need to be watched in any association; these are: your attitude, what you allow people to do to you and masking your apprehension.

1. Attitude is Everything

Attitude is your manner, disposition, feeling, and position with regard to a person or a thing. Your attitude determines your altitude. The Bible tells us that we have the mind of Christ (1 Corinthians 2:16); thus, if your attitude is indeed the posture of your mind and you have the mind of Christ, then your posture to bad company will be to take a stand for Jesus. What is your attitude to wrong or bad suggestions? What is your attitude when you find yourself in a wrong place? What is your attitude when you are drinking what you are not supposed to drink?

Addiction is a learned habit; it takes time to develop. Your attitude could make the habit stick or be stopped immediately. Nehemiah's attitude towards these three evil men was visibly palpable: he refused to do anything with them and that should be our attitude also towards a bad company.

2. What Do You Allow?

Nehemiah was a man full of determination, and ready to do whatever it took to finish the rebuilding of the broken wall. He had the support of the king and his kinsmen who were also ready to engage and complete the task before them. Despite all this support from the king and his people, Nehemiah remained extremely vulnerable and so exposed that he could have easily compromised his stand but he did not allow his adversaries to prevail over him. He stood his ground and prevailed on every side.

The need to be very sensitive in any given relationship is very important because it lays the foundation of what you are going to allow people to do to you or not. Your adversary—which in this context is your addiction—will sometimes plead with you, confront you, or even try to trick you; it is whatever you allow that makes you stand or fall. Anyone can see the handwriting of evil in any relationship but our attitude to it makes it possible for us to tolerate and permit it. If you don't stop evil or any addictive behavior in its track, it will eventually stop you in yours! The question for your consideration is: What are you allowing in your relationship? "Neither give place to the devil." (Ephesians 4:27)

3. Masking Your Apprehension

Nehemiah was very sensitive to his environment. He came to Jerusalem and took time to study the city which he had been away from for at least two decades. He asked questions concerning the welfare of the people; he knew firsthand the attitude of his people towards rebuilding the broken wall; though Sanballat and his friend presented themselves to him as men with the best of intentions, he did not allow their compliments to mask his apprehension towards them. He knew of their plan to delay, derail and destroy the building of the wall—an agenda which is similar to that of any negative addiction—to destroy its host. Anytime you shy away from your inner conviction about anything, it will always result in disaster.

Our apprehension is simply the anticipation of adversity or misfortune; suspicion or fear of future, trouble or evil. Whenever you feel strange about any relationship, please check it out and do not ignore your intuition. Whatever you wait for will always catch up with you! Nehemiah told Sanballat and his friends that they had no part with him *"Then answered I them, and said unto them, The God of heaven, he will prosper us; therefore we his servants will arise and build: but ye have no portion, nor right, nor memorial, in Jerusalem." (Nehemiah 2:20)*

This sounds like a decision we can also make regarding the negative addictions in our lives.

WORDS TO PONDER ON...

"Be ye not equally yoked..."

> *"Be ye not unequally yoked together with unbelievers: for what fellowship hath righteousness with unrighteousness? and what communion hath light with darkness? And what concord hath Christ with Belial? or what part hath he that believeth with an infidel? And what agreement hath the temple of God with idols? for ye are the temple of the living God; as God hath said, I will dwell in them, and walk in them; and I will be their God, and they shall be my people." (2 Corinthians 6:14-16)*

This instruction is pretty clear; we are commanded to avoid any ungodly relationships. Avoidance is the best cure to any addictive behavior! Righteousness will always prevail over unrighteousness, as light will certainly prevail over darkness. We should allow our light to shine as we are instructed in the Bible for we are a city set on a hill that cannot be hidden. Rebuilding from any addictive behavior calls for your total separation from what caused it; if your are unwilling to separate, then you have simply created a revolving door of a life of defeat. You are meant to be a champion, and with God on your side, you can!

ASSIGNMENT

1. Who are the three people you are closest to?

2. What is your attitude towards life in general?

3. What do you allow people to do to you?

4. Do you allow your inner voice to speak?

Day 35

TIME TO EVERY PURPOSE

"And the king said unto me, (the queen also sitting by him,) For how long shall thy journey be? and when wilt thou return? So it pleased the king to send me; and I set him a time." (Nehemiah 2:6)

The king asked Nehemiah the duration of his journey and his anticipated time of return. As simple as these questions sound, they are lifesavers. If you are careful with your time, you will not lose in life. I firmly believe that a life of addiction begins with poor time management, because if you spend your time in a wrong place with the wrong kind of people, the result will be bad!

Moses, in Psalm 90:10, observes that seventy years is the number of years an average man lives for, and if by the reason of strength, eighty years. In other words, an average person lives about 25,550 days. Out of those days, 8,517 is taken away by sleep; so we truly live for about 17,000 days and if we spend our time right, we will not allow any wrong association to rob us of any of those precious days.

Ecclesiastes 3:1 tells us that there is a time to every purpose—a life that must avoid addiction must be a life that has found its purpose. The advent of social media has robbed many of their time here on earth. Lately, there has been an increase in deaths due to the usage of social media while behind the wheel—a new addictive behavior the devil has blessed some people with. Anyone that will waste your time is a silent killer and a destroyer of your God-given purpose. If you ask people with an addiction problem how it started, nine out of ten of them will tell you it began with poor time management—spending time with the wrong crowd. There is a time to cast away stones, and a time to gather stones; a time to embrace, and a time to refrain from embracing (Ecclesiastes 3:5-7)—in fact, to effectively recognize the time and season of your life is the best cure for addiction—sometimes without the need for any medical intervention.

Nehemiah set the time for his purpose and it helped him to focus his attention on what mattered most. He avoided wrong company knowing that he had promised the king when he would return to him. Raising Nehemiahs is all about realizing that we must return to the King on a certain day, after leading a life that fulfilled His purpose—don't allow any addiction rob you of that. Your today determines your tomorrow; live intentionally now, warding off any distraction and being always mindful of how the actions you take today might change the course of your tomorrow.

Tomorrow is your future. Your destiny is in your hand; plan for it. When we manage our time poorly, the tangible and intangible assets of our precious life are stolen from us, making our lives appear trashy. As you rebuild your life from any addiction, remember the Lord will restore the years the cankerworm has eaten. With God on your side, you can do it.

WORDS TO PONDER ON...

"Redeeming the time..."

> *"Redeeming the time, because the days are evil. Wherefore be ye not unwise, but understanding what the will of the Lord is." (Ephesians 5:16-17)*

The word 'redeem' is the root word for 'redemption'. Just like you were redeemed from sin by Christ, you must let God help you with your time management. It takes the grace of God to use your time aright—the same way you were redeemed by grace. If you don't understand the will of God for your life, you will abuse your life. Take it serious from today to redeem your time.

ASSIGNMENT

1. Do you understand the purpose of God for your life?
2. Are you in that purpose for your life?
3. If you are to meet the Lord at seventy, what have you done with your life now?
4. How many days do you have left, assuming seventy is the number of years you will spend on earth? Are you fulfilled?

Day 36

BEING ACCOUNTABLE

"Moreover I said unto the king, If it please the king, let letters be given me to the governors beyond the river, that they may convey me over till I come into Judah; And a letter unto Asaph the keeper of the king's forest, that he may give me timber to make beams for the gates of the palace which pertained to the house, and for the wall of the city, and for the house that I shall enter into. And the king granted me, according to the good hand of my God upon me." (Nehemiah 2:7-8)

Nehemiah was very much ready to build or repair the walls of Jerusalem, the moment Hanani informed him about the situation of the remnants in Jerusalem. However, he needed some supplies to do the work, hence his request to the king for a letter to be given to him so that he might obtain the needed materials for rebuilding the wall. Nehemiah was, from that moment, accountable to the king regarding his time, the supplies and the people back in Jerusalem. His sense of accountability to the king kept his focus on his mission and not allowing his adversaries to stop the work.

Addiction builds its stronghold in any life that is void of accountability. When you feel that you cannot be controlled by anyone, you become an easy target because isolation is the breeding place for life-terminating behaviors.

What does it mean to be accountable to someone? It is to subject to the obligation to report, explain or be responsible to someone; to become answerable to someone. Being accountable has been discarded as an outdated virtue; we now live in an age where independence is the new normal, causing a lot of people to be cut off from the support they so much needed. Even among Christians, it is no longer common to see people committed to being accountable—husbands to wives, fathers to children, mothers to children and pastors to their own congregations.

There are three things I have seen that make being accountable increasingly very difficult: people not knowing what assets are vulnerable when we are not accountable, the unwillingness to follow advice, and the lack of zeal to make the necessary adjustments. An addictive behavior will destroy anyone who cannot confess to someone else about their challenges; after all, addiction is a problem not a sin. James 5:16 exhorts:

> *"Confess your faults one to another, and pray one for another, that ye may be healed. The effectual fervent prayer of a righteous man availeth much."*

1. What Are My Assets?

Assets are worth protecting. Do you have any? Yes you do! I will tell you what they are in a moment. Nehemiah knew what assets he had and protected them very well, even if that meant that he and his people had to build with one hand and carry weapons with the other, doing everything to protect those assets.

What are your assets? The big three are: Time, People and Money. If you are accountable with your time you will never get in trouble. For example, you get paid according to the time on your time sheet because your employer is making sure that the time you said you were at work is accounted for. If we could live our lives like we are getting paid for every minute therein, we would not waste any of it. Spending time in wrong places and leading an unproductive lifestyle would not only decrease but vanish!

People are the most precious things in life; even God wanted our company so much that He created us. Every evening in the cool of the day, He came down and spent time with our first parents. When you live an addictive lifestyle, you are not only destroying yourself but also everyone associated with you. Will you deliberately kill any of your family? The answer is understandably a NO! But every time you are not accountable to them and you choose your addiction over them, you are killing them.

Money, of course, is a valuable asset as well. If you are accountable with your money, you will not spend it on anything that can or will result into an addiction. Does your wife or husband know what you spend on? Can you send your children to get anything you will consume? If God had to ask you to show Him your checkbook, would He be proud of you? When we keep all these in the right perspective, life will be well with us.

2. Unwillingness to Follow Advice

Nehemiah came to Jerusalem, ready to rebuild the broken wall. He had all the supplies he needed to commence the work, but he did not act like he did not need anybody to start the work.

> *"And I arose in the night, I and some few men with me; neither told I any man what my God had put in my heart to do at Jerusalem:*

> *neither was there any beast with me, save the beast that I rode upon." (Nehemiah 2:12)*

Nehemiah arose in the night, not by himself alone, - he had some men with him. While we do not know how many men were there that night, there were at least two of them, justifying the wisdom of the Preacher that two are better than one.

Addiction makes you avoid the very people God has placed in your life to help you get free from that particular problem. Arrogance is a natural byproduct of addiction, making you feel like everyone is beneath your feet. What is the place of advice? An advice is an ornament of grace and a chain about your neck. Proverbs 1:8-9 says,

> *"My son, hear the instruction of thy father, and forsake not the law of thy mother: For they shall be an ornament of grace unto thy head, and chains about thy neck."*

A good advice, taken, will surely beautify your life. Being accountable is opening yourself up to a godly counsel that will lead to the path of righteousness. The good advice you accept today will shape your tomorrow. If the shape of your life is not what you envisioned, then check the source of the advice you are getting or the lack thereof.

3. The Lack of Zeal to Make Adjustments

Nehemiah arose by night with some men and walked by the wall. He needed those men to give him their views and a godly counsel on the way forward. It was quite evident in the later chapters of the book of Nehemiah how he made the necessary adjustments to his strategies on building and completing the walls in fifty-two days.

Addiction does not want you to make any adjustments because making any sensible adjustment means that you are becoming free. If you are not being accountable, you will not be able to recognize your assets, you will not be willing to take any godly advice and, as result, you will not be able to make the necessary adjustments to set you free. He or she that refuses to yield to a godly counsel and does not make the necessary adjustments shall suddenly be destroyed, and that without remedy.

> *"He, that being often reproved hardeneth his neck, shall suddenly be destroyed, and that without remedy." (Proverbs 29:1)*

WORDS TO PONDER ON...

"Everyone shall give account of himself..."

> *"So then every one of us shall give account of himself to God." (Romans 14:12)*

Nehemiah got a letter from the king to pick up what he needed for the work ahead of him. In like manner, each of us has been given talents by God to profit with. Addiction will likely kill any talent that God gives you. We must always keep in mind that one of these days we shall give an account of ourselves to God. If we are going to give an account to God, then we should start practicing here with ourselves. Practice makes perfection; by the time we get before the Master, we will have perfected the act.

ASSIGNMENT

1. Who are you accountable to?

2. What are you doing with your assets?

3. What is the source of the advice shaping your life?

4. Do you find it difficult to adjust?

Day 37

NEGLECTING EVIL BEHAVIOR

"But it came to pass, that when Sanballat heard that we builded the wall, he was wroth, and took great indignation, and mocked the Jews." (Nehemiah 4:1)

The devil wants us to focus on the minor so that we neglect the major. This is the number one strategy of Satan. Once the devil gets our attention away from our main objective, then he can easily cut us off. Nehemiah was focused on the wall, but his adversaries were more focused on mockery, telling him that the quality of the work performed was substandard. Addiction is a stronghold and spirit that cannot be neglected or discounted as something that could be easily overcome by willpower alone.

What does it mean to neglect? To neglect is paying no attention or too little attention to something or someone; it is to disregard or slight; to omit, through indifference or carelessness. What the devil wants from the life of an addict is to not pay any attention to the problem—to be indifferent and careless with it.

There are three ways the devil accomplishes this task. One, the devil wants us to neglect our great salvation. When we neglect our salvation which was bought by the blood of Jesus and given to us on the platform of grace, then the question is; How shall we escape from the hold of addiction? As the Scripture says,

> *"How shall we escape, if we neglect so great salvation; which at the first began to be spoken by the Lord, and was confirmed unto us by them that heard him" (Hebrews 2:3).*

Jesus paid the price for your deliverance, and it is never late for you. I declare unto you that this is your time!

The second strategy the devil uses to accomplish this is to make us to forsake or neglect the assembling of ourselves together. He discourages you from fellowshipping with other Christians knowing that once you are cut off, then the addiction becomes capable of incapacitating you. The Bible encourages us in Isaiah 40:31,

> *"They that wait upon the Lord shall renew their strength; they shall mount up with wings as eagles; they shall run, and not be weary; and they shall walk, and not faint."*

This is what happens when we come to the Lord for help in fellowship; it will help you to neglect every evil behavior and addictions. This is why the Scripture further says,

> *"Not forsaking the assembling of ourselves together, as the manner of some is; but exhorting one another: and so much the more, as ye see the day approaching." (Hebrews 10:25)*

The third strategy is to keep you lukewarm—neither hot nor cold—and that creates a big problem between you and God. This is what an addictive behavior turns a beautiful life into—a life unfulfilled. Addiction keeps you up one day and down the other; the life of an addicted person becomes like a yo-yo that never finds a balance. God spews people with such a lifestyle out of His mouth. He says in Revelation 3:15-16,

> *"I know thy works, that thou art neither cold nor hot: I would thou wert cold or hot. So then because thou art lukewarm, and neither cold nor hot, I will spue thee out of my mouth."*

God so loved the world that He sent Jesus just for you, to deliver you from this up-today-and-down-tomorrow lifestyle; it is time to rebuild this beautiful life of yours!

WORDS TO PONDER ON...

"Have no fellowship..."

> *"And have no fellowship with the unfruitful works of darkness, but rather reprove them." (Ephesians 5:11)*

This instruction in the context of Ephesians 5:11 is pretty clear. We are to have no relationship with any form of negative addiction. To have fellowship with the unfruitful works of darkness means engaging wrong people at a wrong time and at a wrong place. Addiction can be cured by heeding these simple admonitions. Of course, these do not substitute for medical attention and counseling if and when required, but that will amount to putting a bandaid on a major wound if these principles are not adhered to.

ASSIGNMENT

1. Are you born again?

2. Are you still in fellowship with Christ?

3. Do you attend a local church?
4. Are you a volunteer at your church?

Day 38

HEALTH MATTERS

"And they said unto me, The remnant that are left of the captivity there in the province are in great affliction and reproach: the wall of Jerusalem also is broken down, and the gates thereof are burned with fire." (Nehemiah 1:3)

Health issues are very real, more so now that we live in a world of genetically altered, processed and fast foods. The incidence of people getting ill is at an alarming rate and the need to address our health issues is not only necessary but urgent and important. Nehemiah was told about the deplorable condition of the people in Jerusalem; the economy was not in good shape, relationship with God was non-existent and the health of the people was in chaos. Many relationships, businesses, families and careers have been destroyed because of a major illness, so the need to rebuild after an episode of illness must be addressed with all sincerity.

There are many diseases in the world today, as it was in the days of

Jesus Christ. Of His days, we read that He healed palsy, blindness, issue of blood, fever and other ailments that could have not been mentioned. The Bible tells us that He healed them all and He is still healing today through His word, because Jesus is the word of God. You are probably familiar with the story of the woman with the issue of blood who had spent all she had on physicians; the man that laid at the pool of Bethesda for thirty eight years; blind Bartimaeus; the man sick of palsy whose friends carried to the rooftop, and so on. These were people with damaging and crippling experiences, but as earlier stated in previous chapters, whatever has been lost could and will be restored in Jesus' name. Whatever has been lost could be rebuilt with the principles or suggestions made in the previous chapters - whether it is your relationship, career, business, family, or regarding a negative addiction.

It is very important to know how we can build our health and vitality back after an illness. While I am not an expert in the area of nutrition or medicine—since my calling is in the area of physical therapy which I am very good at—however, I have been able to identify five things that could hasten our restoration. They are: application of the word, the use of medication, diet, exercise, prayer and fasting. Congratulations to some of us that are healthy. My advice is that you continue with what has kept you healthy and if you ever find yourself under attack, then you will know what to do.

APPLICATION OF THE WORD

"Jesus healed them all!" The good news is that He is still the same yesterday, today and forever, so Jesus will heal all our diseases as He has promised in His word. The Bible reveals to us in John 1:1 that

"In the beginning was the Word, and the Word was with God, and the Word was God."

Jesus releases the healing virtue to us by the revelation of His Word. *"He sent his word, and healed them, and delivered them from their destructions." (Psalms 107:20)* Everything about your healing is forever settled in His Word.

The good thing about God sending His Word is that He sends His Word on your behalf to whosoever needs to be involved in your wellbeing. Perhaps, you've heard someone say to you before, "you have been on my mind all day". My friend, that's God sending His memo on your behalf. Anyone that has anything to do with your financial, emotional, physical and social wellbeing will be receiving a Word to get involved with you and that's the beauty of allowing God to be at the center of your life. He knows what is best for you and who can do it well.

If you are dealing with depression, it is revealed in the Bible that *"a merry heart does good like medicine"! (Proverbs 17:22)* To apply the Word, we must look at or do things that make our heart merry—things like worshipping, listening to godly comedy or whatever lifts your spirit.

If you are dealing with insomnia, we know that He promised us in His Word that *"He gives His beloved sleep" (Psalms 127:2)* Those are some examples. Remember, He upholds all things (including all things pertaining to you) by the Word of His power. We must be the students of the Word so that we can take personal responsibilities for the outcomes of our lives

PRAYER AND FASTING FOR HEALING

Prayer and fasting works all day and every day. Jesus Himself prayed for many and virtue came out of His body. It is through prayer that we communicate our needs to God. He has promised that He will answer our prayers and we have been encouraged to ask, seek and knock for answers to our everyday problems (Matthew 7:7). These include our health matters. Jesus emphasized the effect of fasting for answers when He said to his disciples after a failed attempt to cast out an evil spirit from an oppressed lad, *"Howbeit this kind goeth not out but by prayer and fasting." (Matthew 17:21)*

During fasting, we undergo both physical and spiritual cleansing. And the same is true medically. When doctors desire to get meaningful results from their patient's body system, the patient is always told to abstain from food (hence, fasting reduces blood sugar level for instance). Likewise, the usual pre-op medical instruction given to patients that are about to undergo surgery is NPO (which means 'nothing per oral'). If fasting reveals so much about our health, then fasting must be a tool that can be used to treat some of our problems. A weekly fasting is not only to ask God for what we need but also for inner cleansing. Note however that fasting must be done under your physician's guidance, and if your health permits. Jesus had a very healthy lifestyle, but He also lived a fasted life

THE USE OF MEDICATION

The need for modern medicine to help with the management of our medical issues cannot be overemphasized, but our God wants us to bring everything to Him first. The main reason why God wants us to come to Him is simply this: most of the time we see only with our physical eyes, and sometimes our problem is not physical but spiritual. The Bible in Psalm 91, talks about the arrows that fly by day and pestilence that wastes at noonday—those are direct attacks from the kingdom of darkness that do not respond to modern medicine. We also need God's direction and divine guidance on who to choose and where to go to receive the best care.

God is not against physicians but we have seen in the scripture that He gets very displeased when He is not consulted about our decisions even regarding our choice of medical provider. The story of King Asa was a perfect example of not seeking God first before choosing a physician.

> *"And Asa in the thirty and ninth year of his reign was diseased in his feet, until his disease was exceeding great: yet in his disease he sought not to the Lord, but to the physicians." (2 Chronicles 16:12)*

Now let us look at several examples in the Bible where the use of medication or seeing a physician is in line with the word of God. Jesus talks about the woman with the issue of blood who who had visited physicians for twelve years without any result; He did not rebuke her for seeing them! Isaiah talks about the use of ointment for treatment of certain illnesses (Isaiah 1:6). Jesus also talked about the Good Samaritan who brought the man into an inn (hospital) to be treated with oil and wine (Luke 10:34). Even Jesus spat into the soil and made mud which He then applied to the eyes of a blind man.

There are lots of vitamins and supplements in the marketplace to help your health, but most importantly, you need God to guide you to someone who will point you in the right direction on what vitamins and supplements are best for your system. God is the creator of all herbs and they are meant to be used for eating and medicinal purposes. If you are sick, consult the God of heaven for His direction to who will best take care of you. As you choose your medical provider, may the good Lord give you divine guidance.

EFFECTIVE DIET

In Genesis 1, God created many things, of which food is of the utmost importance. He created both herbs and animals for our consumption on the third and the fourth day. Humans to consume the food were created on the sixth day. This tells us that God had our daily provision in mind even before we ever showed up! He gave every herb and the beasts to us for food and He gave us control over them. (Genesis 1:11-13, 19-21, 29-30) Unfortunately, food has taken the dominion that God gave in the lives of many and, as a result, sickness and ill health abound.

The use of effective diet to improve your health is of utmost importance because without proper amount of good nutrition you can get very sick. There are different types of diets in the world today. My sincere advice is for you to consult someone with good knowledge of your health issues for the kind of dieting instructions that suit your condition. From the scriptures we have seen or read about different kinds of diet, such as God's diet, Daniel's diet, and John the Baptist kind of diet. One vital instruction remains a golden piece of advice to anyone that wants to live a healthy lifestyle, and that is: do all things in moderation! (Philippians 4:5) Proverbs 25:16 clearly says,

> *"Hast thou found honey? eat so much as is sufficient for thee, lest thou be filled therewith, and vomit it."*

EFFECTIVE EXERCISE

The lack of exercise in our daily routine has now become an epidemic that requires a quick and divine intervention. Our lifestyle has become more dependent on machines than at any other time in history. We drive through to order our food, we let washing machines do our laundry, we drive through at the bank, we jump into elevators at work and can catch a shuttle almost everywhere. As a result we have become a very sick society at large as our lack of exercise has invited all manner of health conditions. The need for exercise in our daily routine is a subject we can no longer push aside but must confront head-on. Paul told Timothy, "bodily exercise profits a little..." (1 Timothy 4:8). He could as well be saying that to modern day believers!

Paul was comparing physical exercise to a spiritual one, hence the qualification, 'little'; but there's no doubt that there is a tremendous amount of help our body receives when we exercise regularly. In the Old Testament, we read about Enoch, Moses, Noah, Lot and many more who lived in sound health and lived over one hundred years. One thing was common to them, apart from serving God, and eating natural food, they all walked everywhere!

The story of Jonah comes readily to mind. When God initially instructed him to go and tell the people of Nineveh to repent of their sins, he rebelled. However, when he finally decided to obey God, he traveled on foot for a three-day journey into the city (Jonah 3:3-4). Jesus traveled everywhere on foot. I am fully aware that we now live in an advanced world where the need to be mobile to do more for God is important, but at the same time we should not forsake regular bodily exercise, lest (like many other Christians) we go home too soon.

We need to allow for exercises in our daily schedule so that we can fulfill our purpose here on earth. Acts 7:38 refers to the mass exodus of the children of Israel from Egypt to Canaan as the church in the wilderness; they also walked from Egypt to the Promised Land. God could have translated them from Egypt to Canaan but they walked!

My best guess is that they needed the exercise, after all they had eaten in Egypt (just kidding). But think about it; after walking that long, they remained healthy—not even their legs were swollen, nor did any of them appear feeble.

> *"Yea, forty years didst thou sustain them in the wilderness, so that they lacked nothing; their clothes waxed not old, and their feet swelled not." (Nehemiah 9:21)*

Exercise is God's prescription for our health. He modeled this for us by coming in the cool of the day to walk with Adam and Eve in the garden; He expects the New Testament church to exercise as well.

WORDS TO PONDER ON...

"The balm in Gilead..."

> *"Is there no balm in Gilead; is there no physician there? why then is not the health of the daughter of my people recovered?"(Jeremiah 8:22)*

Jesus is the balm in Gilead, and our spiritual medicine. If you have challenges with your health, then you must go to the Healer, and when you do your health will be recovered. There's still a balm in Gilead, and He's now your personal physician, therefore your health must recover.

ASSIGNMENT

1. How often do you read the Word?
2. Are you on medication? Are you using it faithfully?
3. Are you on any diet?

4. How often do you exercise?

5. How often do you fast?

Day 39

ENEMIES OF PROGRESS

"But when Sanballat the Horonite, and Tobiah the servant, the Ammonite, and Geshem the Arabian, heard it, they laughed us to scorn, and despised us, and said, What is this thing that ye do? will ye rebel against the king?" (Nehemiah 2:19)

WHO WAS SANBALLAT?

Nehemiah was in captivity when the report about the condition of the wall of Jerusalem was delivered to him by his friend, Hanani. He had every reason not to care about the affairs of the remnant or the condition in Jerusalem—for one, and quite importantly, he was not a free man; he was under authority as the king's cupbearer in a different empire. The time was not right, the circumstances were not perfect, the resources needed were not available, but Nehemiah engaged with the rebuilding of the wall anyway.

There's never a perfect time or scenario to start building or rebuilding; there will always be obstacles, oppositions and discouragement, even when it is the appointed time to arise and build. Nehemiah encountered three difficult personalities—terrible individuals—who were bent on frustrating efforts to rebuild the wall of Jerusalem. These men were Sanballat, Tobiah, and Geshem—men of negative influence! These were the enemies Nehemiah encountered in his days; unfortunately, their likes are still very much around today.

Who was Sanballat? Sanballat simply means an ENEMY IN SECRET! He appeared to Nehemiah as a man willing to help—a noble man—but he was full of venom and was secretly attacking Nehemiah. Whenever we decide to build or rebuild our lives, there are unforeseen enemies that want to contest with us, but we are rest assured that victory is ours. Are we fighting the enemies in the secret today? Yes! The Bible tells us that we have enemies

in the secret—invisible forces of darkness. Jesus said "Behold I have given you authority to trample on serpents and scorpions and to overcome all the power of the enemy." The serpents and scorpions are the spirit of Sanballat, the enemy in secret. Ephesians 6:12 gives us clarity on what the Sanballat spirit looks like in present day; it says that

> *"For we wrestle not against flesh and blood, but against principalities, against powers, against the rulers of the darkness of this world, against spiritual wickedness in high places."*

The enemies you cannot see cannot be defeated with conventional weapons; therefore we need to engage this type of warfare from the spirit realm by the help of the Holy Spirit. The Bible tells us that

> *"For though we walk in the flesh, we do not war after the flesh: (For*

the weapons of our warfare are not carnal, but mighty through God to the pulling down of strongholds;)" (2 Corinthians 10:3-4)

Our enemy cannot be fought physically but spiritually. Our weapons of warfare are not carnal, but mighty through God to pull down strongholds! Later in the chapters to come we will see the need to pull down strongholds, because once the devil gets you off from building the life you want, then he has successfully taken you to the valley of Ono. You are not alone; with God, all things are possible. Nehemiah defeated Sanballat, Jesus also did—and Christ in you is the hope of glory! Your victory is sure. *"Behold, I give unto you power to tread on serpents and scorpions, and over all the power of the enemy: and nothing shall by any means hurt you." (Luke 10:19)*

WORDS TO PONDER ON...

"There are many adversaries..."

"For a great door and effectual is opened unto me, and there are many adversaries." (1 Corinthians 16:9)

Paul, an apostle of Jesus Christ, experienced this spirit of Sanballat. In one of his letters, he said a great and effectual door had been opened unto him, but he was having difficulty walking through the open door. Why? Because there were many adversaries—invisible forces of darkness. Guess what? Paul had a very successful ministry, and so shall you. Get up, despite these many oppositions, and build or rebuild the life you want!.

ASSIGNMENT

1. Who is the real enemy?
2. How do you fight an enemy you cannot see?
3. Write your recent experience about spiritual warfare

Day 40

WHO WAS TOBIAH?

"But it came to pass, that when Sanballat, and Tobiah, and the Arabians, and the Ammonites, and the Ashdodites, heard that the walls of Jerusalem were made up, and that the breaches began to be stopped, then they were very wroth." (Nehemiah 4:7)

WHO WAS TOBIAH?

Nehemiah took time to study his enemies. He understood their mode of attack, their time of attack, the style of their attack, and the weapon of their attack. In like manner, his enemies took time to study Nehemiah, looking for his moment of weakness, weariness and carelessness. Our enemies are busier than ever, looking out for our moment of weakness, watching our every move so as to do us harm. The enemies are also not unaware that it might be difficult to defeat you alone; hence Sanballat and Tobiah teamed up to launch an attack on Nehemiah.

The Bible encourages us to be watchful and prayerful so as to understand the strategies of our adversaries. Tobiah was one of the enemies that wanted the rebuilding of the wall to stop. He used all his influence and power to attack Nehemiah, but he was not successful against him.

Who was Tobiah? Tobiah simply means CAMOUFLAGE. To camouflage is the act or result of obscuring things to deceive an opponent. It also means to fake, give false appearance or set up a smokescreen or a disguise. The adversary wants to catch us unawares by presenting himself as a friend rather than the sworn enemy that he is. He wants to disguise as a lion, knowing that Jesus is the Lion of Judah, so he roars like a lion even though he is not a lion. Apostle Paul encourages us to keep our eyes wide open about false apostles—deceitful workers who are camouflaging as apostles of Christ. Even Satan himself transforms himself into an angel of light. It is very important to know the word of God thoroughly so that we can detect the wiles of the enemies. Jesus warned us against false prophets, which come to us in sheep's clothing, but inwardly are ravening wolves—what a disguise and a terrible camouflage!

> *"For such are false apostles, deceitful workers, transforming themselves into the apostles of Christ. And no marvel; for Satan himself is transformed into an angel of light. Therefore it is no great thing if his ministers also be transformed as the ministers of righteousness; whose end shall be according to their works." (2 Corinthians 11:13-15)*

Let us look at a story in Joshua 9 about the Gibeonites, enemy of the Israelites who disguised as friends. They successfully deceived Joshua and his men, tricked them to a treaty that later became a thorn in the flesh for the children of Israel.

> *"And when the inhabitants of Gibeon heard what Joshua had done unto Jericho and to Ai, They did work wilily, and went and made as*

if they had been ambassadors, and took old sacks upon their asses, and wine bottles, old, and rent, and bound up; And old shoes and clouted upon their feet, and old garments upon them; and all the bread of their provision was dry and mouldy. And they went to Joshua unto the camp at Gilgal, and said unto him, and to the men of Israel, We be come from a far country: now therefore make ye a league with us." (Joshua 9:3-6)

We need watchful eyes and divine intelligence to detect these terrible enemies. When Sanballat (enemy in secret) and Tobiah (camouflage) come together to attack, if we are not watchful, the effect of such an attack could affect us severely. The need to team up with other believers becomes significantly important to destroy these terrible enemies.

Nehemiah had to confront the spirit of Tobiah with the help of the Spirit of God. The good news is that we have a better covenant and better promises than Nehemiah; so we also must confront the spirit of Tobiah and, with the help of the Holy Spirit Who knows all things, we will overcome the spirit of Tobiah successfully.

"Beware of false prophets, which come to you in sheep's clothing, but inwardly they are ravening wolves." (Matthew 7:15)

WORDS TO PONDER ON...

"The Spirit searches all things..."

"But God hath revealed them unto us by his Spirit: for the Spirit searcheth all things, yea, the deep things of God." (1 Corinthians 2:10)

No enemy can hide from God and that same God has given us His Spirit—the Holy Spirit—and that Spirit knows all things, even what the devil is planning at the moment. The Holy Spirit talks to us—He speaks by intuition, conviction, whispering to your spirit man and through the written word of God. We listen to His voice to our own advantage.

ASSIGNMENT

1. Do you have any knowledge of the enemy's disguise?
2. What was the last trick the enemy played on you?
3. Do you understand spiritual warfare?
4. What are the weapons available to believers?

Day 41

WHO WAS GESHEM?

"That Sanballat and Geshem sent unto me, saying, Come, let us meet together in some one of the villages in the plain of Ono. But they thought to do me mischief." (Nehemiah 6:2)

WHO WAS GESHEM?

Nehemiah was always battle ready. He never allowed himself to be distracted; rather he kept his eyes on the end result which was to rebuild the broken wall of Jerusalem. Sanballat (enemy in secret) and Tobiah (camouflage) did everything possible to get Nehemiah off the wall; he was bullied, threatened and offered a compromise but he prevailed by his willingness to follow God's plans wholly. Since Sanballat and Tobiah could not prevail against Nehemiah, they brought another weapon to fight him—Geshem. Learning from Nehemiah, we also must be battle ready always. The Bible encourages us to put on the whole armor of God because it will take the whole armor to defeat the devil that wants to stop you from building or rebuilding the life you truly want.

Who was Geshem? Geshem simply means THE FLOOD. That phrase should sound familiar to you, because this is one of the best kept secrets of the devil. When the devil has tried everything against you and nothing is working, then the devil comes in like a flood in the spirit of Geshem. Prophet Isaiah reveals to us that the enemy may choose to come in like a flood and the antidote is that the Spirit of the Lord shall lift up a standard against him. *"So shall they fear the name of the Lord from the west, and his glory from the rising of the sun. When the enemy shall come in like a flood, the Spirit of the Lord shall lift up a standard against him." (Isaiah 59:19)*

So this spirit of Geshem comes to overpower, and sweep people off their feet. Without a solid foundation on the solid rock—which is Jesus—this spirit will overcome anyone.

Let us consider two examples of what a flood-attack looks like. One is in Matthew 27 where all the chief priests and elders of the people took counsel against Jesus to put Him to death—talk about a flood of an attack! Pilate released a notable criminal called Barabbas instead of an innocent man, and from there on everything went bad for Jesus until He was crucified. (To get the full picture, please read the Matthew 27 and 28).

> *"When the morning was come, all the chief priests and elders of the people took counsel against Jesus to put him to death:And they had then a notable prisoner, called Barabbas. Then released he Barabbas unto them: and when he had scourged Jesus, he delivered him to be crucified." (Matthew 27:1, 16, 26)*

While some might argue that Jesus was able to take all that because He was both fully human and fully God at the same time, our second case study was not. Paul was a man like us who was also saved by grace, but we read in the scriptures the numerous afflictions that came upon him in his ministry. A perfect picture of a flood of attack against him was painted in 2 Corinthians 11:24-28. The spirit of Geshem is a terrible spirit employed by the devil to sweep us off our feet, but rest assured that victory is sure in Jesus.

> *"Of the Jews five times received I forty stripes save one. Thrice was I beaten with rods, once was I stoned, thrice I suffered shipwreck, a night and a day I have been in the deep; In journeyings often, in perils of waters, in perils of robbers, in perils by mine own countrymen, in perils by the heathen, in perils in the city, in perils in the wilderness, in perils in the sea, in perils among false brethren; In weariness and painfulness, in watchings often, in hunger and thirst, in fastings often, in cold and nakedness. Beside those things that are without, that which cometh upon me daily, the care of all the churches." (2 Corinthians 11:24-28)*

WORDS TO PONDER ON...

"What shall separate us from the love of Christ?"

> *"Who shall separate us from the love of Christ? shall tribulation, or distress, or persecution, or famine, or nakedness, or peril, or sword?"(Romans 8:35)*

As you mature in the things of God, the enemy takes notice and attacks you like a flood but you are too strong to be taken down as such. In any case, the spirit of Geshem is alive and well, hence, we are admonished "whom you resist steadfastly…" (1 Peter 5:9) and that is the only weapon to stop this wicked spirit.

ASSIGNMENT

1. What is your experience with this type of spirit?
2. Do you now understand the reason why certain things happen?
3. Can you now relate better with someone going through this kind of attacks?
4. Has this improved your view about spiritual warfare?

Day 42

THE PLAINS OF ONO

"That Sanballat and Geshem sent unto me, saying, Come, let us meet together in some one of the villages in the plain of Ono. But they thought to do me mischief." (Nehemiah 6:2)

A PLACE OF BARGAINING AND STRONGHOLD

Nehemiah was diligent and determined to see the wall of Jerusalem completely rebuilt. There were many adversaries against this mission; those that were hell bent on stopping the rebuilders from rebuilding the wall. We fight the same enemies today, and their singular mission is to get us to abandon building or rebuilding our lives. Sanballat and Geshem sent a message to Nehemiah to come and meet in one of the villages in the plain of Ono. They came five times with the same invitation, but Nehemiah resisted and refused to come down from rebuilding the wall. We must understand that our enemies, like Nehemiah's, do not take no for an answer. We need to constantly fight to stay focused on our mission.

> *"Now it came to pass, when Sanballat, and Tobiah, and Geshem the Arabian, and the rest of our enemies, heard that I had builded the wall, and that there was no breach left therein; (though at that time I had not set up the doors upon the gates;) That Sanballat and Geshem sent unto me, saying, Come, let us meet together in some one of the villages in the plain of Ono. But they thought to do me mischief. And I sent messengers unto them, saying, I am doing a great work, so that I cannot come down: why should the work cease, whilst I leave it, and come down to you? Yet they sent unto me four times after this sort; and I answered them after the same manner."(Nehemiah 6:1-4)*

Let us look at what that invitation really meant. What does Ono mean? On the surface it simply means "ON THE NEAREST OFFER". The enemy wants to bargain with our lives by offering us alternatives to our main goal. For example, imagine that you are about to reconcile with your spouse; it is not unlikely that the devil will begin to remind you of what you will be missing by making the reconciliation—how, for instance, you might not be able to continue to see others like you were doing before the reconciliation. Anytime we allow the devil to bargain with us, we can never win because he has all the resources to outwit you. If he tried it with Jesus in the wildernesses, you can be assured that he will try it with you.

The most important meaning of Ono is 'the land of STRONGHOLDS'. The end result of the enemy's plan is to bait us to the plain of Ono, by bargaining with our future, and once we are there, to lock us down with chains until the hold is so strong that we become ensnared. Strongholds cannot just be ignored or pacified; they must be pulled down and that requires a lot of work and spiritual warfare. It is better to avoid the bargaining power of the devil by all means necessary than to be dealing with the strongholds. There are six tactics of the enemy in this regard that I have identified for us to consider. They include:

1. Mockery
2. Anger and conspiracy
3. Tiredness and loss of vigor
4. Fear,
5. Propaganda
6. False prophecy and distractions

We will consider them one after the other in the next few chapters. Happy reading.

WORDS TO PONDER ON...

"We are not ignorant of our enemy's devices…"

> *"Lest Satan should get an advantage of us: for we are not ignorant of his devices." (2 Corinthians 2:11)*

The devil is doing everything within his power to take advantage of us—and expectedly so. He does this by engaging us in a bargain for our future but for us to overcome his power, we have to be conversant with his tactics, which—as we have pointed out in this chapter—are bargaining and establishing strongholds.

ASSIGNMENT

1. When was the last time the devil used his weapons on you?
2. What is the devil bargaining for in your life?
3. Do you know have a better understanding of these tactics?
4. Does this now make you a better warrior?

Day 43

TACTIC #1: MOCKERY

"But when Sanballat the Horonite, and Tobiah the servant, the Ammonite, and Geshem the Arabian, heard it, they laughed us to scorn, and despised us, and said, What is this thing that ye do? will ye rebel against the king?" (Nehemiah 2:19)

The enemy has many lethal weapons that he wants to use against us, and he will not hesitate to use any of them if we allow him to step into our affairs. Nehemiah understood and fought against this weapon, and he prevailed by the help of the Spirit of the Lord. The first of these weapons of choice is mockery and if it was used against Nehemiah, rest assured that the enemy will use it against us. Sanballat, Tobiah and Geshem laughed Nehemiah to scorn, and despised him. Sanballat mocked everyone helping Nehemiah; he even called them feeble and called their sincerity to question.

"But it came to pass, that when Sanballat heard that we builded the wall, he was wroth, and took great indignation, and mocked the Jews.

> *And he spake before his brethren and the army of Samaria, and said, What do these feeble Jews? will they fortify themselves? will they sacrifice? will they make an end in a day? will they revive the stones out of the heaps of the rubbish which are burned? Now Tobiah the Ammonite was by him, and he said, Even that which they build, if a fox go up, he shall even break down their stone wall." (Nehemiah 4:1-3)*

It's interesting that this same weapon was used against Jesus.

> *"And the men that held Jesus mocked him, and smote him. And when they had blindfolded him, they struck him on the face, and asked him, saying, Prophesy, who is it that smote thee? And many other things blasphemously spake they against him." (Luke 22:63-65)*

The account of Luke about Jesus revealed that He was mocked many times, He was blindfolded, they struck Him in the face, and asked Him to prophesy unto them. Just picture the scene for a moment—the man that came for their redemption and did many miracles amongst them, now being mocked in the most embarrassing way conceivable? The devil uses this tactic of mockery to break your spirit while you are busy building or rebuilding your life; so watch out for the naysayers, doomsdayers, finger pointers, backbiters, critics and demoralizers—they are everywhere and they are the present day manifestation of the spirit of Sanballat, Tobiah and Geshem. Don't allow them to limit your power to conquer.

WORDS TO PONDER ON...

"The scoffers..."

> *"Knowing this first, that there shall come in the last days scoffers, walking after their own lusts." (2 Peter 3:3)*

Scoffers, mockers—call them whatever you like—but the devil will send them our way in these last days for one purpose only: to derail us from building or rebuilding the life we want according to God's design. Beware.

ASSIGNMENT

1. Do a complete assessment of the people in your sphere of influence
2. Do you have anyone within your circle who is a mocker?
3. What do I do with them?
4. Are you ready to confront this wicked spirit?

Day 44

TACTIC #2: ANGER AND CONSPIRACY

"But it came to pass, that when Sanballat, and Tobiah, and the Arabians, and the Ammonites, and the Ashdodites, heard that the walls of Jerusalem were made up, and that the breaches began to be stopped, then they were very wroth, And conspired all of them together to come and to fight against Jerusalem, and to hinder it." (Nehemiah 4:7-8)

Despite all the mockery and despising the builders of the wall, Nehemiah remained on the wall and refused to meet in the village at the plain of Ono; so the enemy deployed the next line of attack, which was a combination of anger and conspiracy to stop Nehemiah from completing the wall.

The enemy is still in the habit of deploying these same tricks. When you refuse to be mocked and remain dedicated to your resolve of building or rebuilding your life, the anger of the adversaries is released towards you. Have you noticed that when you refuse to listen to people that have been advising you to do contrary to God's will, their counsel sometimes takes on the tone of anger and conspiracy about your unwillingness to be like them? Even Jesus, the author and finisher of our faith, faced the same spirit when He came before Pilate to be judged because of false allegations levelled against Him—that He was perverting the nation, forbidding people to give to Caesar and saying that He was Christ the king. After a careful examination of the available facts by Pilate, he found nothing against Jesus. As the story unfolds, we could read of how their mockery suddenly became anger; they became very fierce!

> *"And the whole multitude of them arose, and led him unto Pilate. And they began to accuse him, saying, We found this fellow perverting the nation, and forbidding to give tribute to Caesar, saying that he himself is Christ a King. And Pilate asked him, saying, Art thou the King of the Jews? And he answered him and said, Thou sayest it. Then said Pilate to the chief priests and to the people, I find no fault in this man. And they were the more fierce, saying, He stirreth up the people, teaching throughout all Judaea, beginning from Galilee to this place." (Luke 23:1-5)*

If this was done to Jesus, you can expect that the same will be done to you, after all, it is another failing strategy of the enemy and we are not ignorant of his devices; we are more than conquerors.

WORDS TO PONDER ON...

"Be sober, be vigilant..."

> *"Be sober, be vigilant; because your adversary the devil, as a roaring lion, walketh about, seeking whom he may devour:" (1 Peter 5:8)*

The devil is all out against us doing the best with our lives. He hates to see us building or rebuilding our future; he keeps walking about looking for the slightest opportunity to scare us to a halt with his anger. Do not allow him to devour you. Yes, he's always seeking who to devour, but you can always abide in the secret place—under the shadow of the Almighty (Psalm 91:1).

ASSIGNMENT

1. Are you experiencing the challenge discussed here in your life?
2. Do you have friends that suddenly turned their back at you?
3. Do you feel like you are alone?
4. What can you do today about this enemy?

Day 45

TACTIC #3: TIREDNESS AND LOSS OF VIGOR

"And Judah said, The strength of the bearers of burdens is decayed, and there is much rubbish; so that we are not able to build the wall." (Nehemiah 4:10)

Part of the goals of the enemy is to throw rubble or rubbish along our way, so that our strength wanes. They did the same against Nehemiah after they had mocked and scorned and unleashed their anger against the builders of the wall. And this time, they succeeded because with these two tactics combined, the willingness and commitment of the builders waned and for a moment the project stopped. The adversaries said to them ten times that they were coming to destroy everything they had done so far and the builders got tired.

Sometimes in our battle to build or rebuild our lives we get weary and discouraged and often almost retreat from advancing towards our goal. Perhaps, Nehemiah remembered the word of the wise one:

> *"If thou faint in the day of adversity, thy strength is small." (Proverbs 24:10)*

He must have known that *"many are the afflictions of the righteous but the Lord delivers him from them all." (Psalms 34:19)*

It is not a sin to get tired or discouraged; even Jesus felt the same. He was mocked, despised, ridiculed, spat on, had the anger of his adversaries unleashed on Him, beaten beyond recognition and yet He was still required to carry His own cross to the place of crucifixion. He got so tired that God sent Him help by the hand of Simon of Cyrene, who helped Him carry the cross for the rest of the way.

> *"And they compel one Simon a Cyrenian, who passed by, coming out of the country, the father of Alexander and Rufus, to bear his cross. And they bring him unto the place Golgotha, which is, being interpreted, The place of a skull." (Mark 15:21-22)*

When we get discouraged because of the attack of the enemies, all we need to do is ask for God's help and it will come speedily. We cannot turn back from the fight, nor retreat because we are discouraged. As Jesus said, if you lay your hand on the plough and look back, you are not fit for the Kingdom (Luke 9:62).

Nehemiah came to rebuild on the king's order, and he must return to that kingdom with the news that the wall has been completed. Sounds like our story, too, doesn't it? God is cheering us on, our space is reserved in His Kingdom. Nobody can take our crown, so we cannot stop fighting.

> *"They that wait upon the Lord shall renew their strength; they shall mount up with wings as eagles…" (Isaiah 40:31)*

Get in the presence of God for new infusion of divine strength.

WORDS TO PONDER ON...

"God faints not, neither is He weary..."

> *"Hast thou not known? hast thou not heard, that the everlasting God, the Lord, the Creator of the ends of the earth, fainteth not, neither is weary? there is no searching of his understanding." (Isaiah 40:28)*

When you get on God's side, your strength comes from the everlasting God. Everlasting means He will outlast every adversary that comes against you; all you need to do is to wait upon the Lord!

ASSIGNMENT

1. Do you feel like you are fighting alone?
2. Do you feel like you are running out of gas?
3. Do you feel alone?
4. Are you overwhelmed by the circumstances facing you?

Day 46

TACTIC #4: FEAR OF THE ADVERSARY

You've probably heard the saying, "Fear is False Evidence Appearing Real." How true! Being mocked and despised will take a toll on anybody; anger and conspiracy will make anyone tired enough to consider quitting. The usual response to all of these is fear. Fear is the default human response when we become overwhelmed with our situation. Nehemiah and his men were bullied severely and at one point, they abandoned the work. But Nehemiah encouraged his men to fight; they had their swords, spears, bows in one hand and continued building with the other.

> *"Therefore set I in the lower places behind the wall, and on the higher places, I even set the people after their families with their swords, their spears, and their bows. And I looked, and rose up, and said unto the nobles, and to the rulers, and to the rest of the people, Be not ye afraid of them: remember the Lord, which is great and terrible, and fight for your brethren, your sons, and your daughters, your wives, and your houses. And it came to pass, when our enemies heard that it was known unto us, and God had brought their counsel to nought, that we returned all of us to the wall, every one unto his work.So neither*

> *I, nor my brethren, nor my servants, nor the men of the guard which followed me, none of us put off our clothes, saving that everyone put them off for washing." (Nehemiah 4:13-15, 23)*

Some Bible scholars tell us that there are three hundred and sixty five "fear nots" in the Bible—one for each day of the year! God knows that the strategy of the devil with fear is to paralyze our every move until we come to a stand-still, but friend, we must keep fighting the good fight of faith, because the devil is not going to let us build or rebuild the life we want.

David had the same experience. He wrote,

> *"though I walk through the valley of shadow of death, I will fear no evil." (Psalms 23:4)*

As long you keep going towards the goal, you have nothing to fear because God is with you. Fear is not a new strategy and has been defeated many times in the Bible. When the children of Israel were at the Red Sea, with Pharaoh's army charging behind, it seemed as though everything had come to an end for them, they became afraid and thought the end had come; but God showed up and instructed Moses on the way forward. Moses said unto the people,

> *"Fear ye not, stand still, and see the salvation of the Lord, which he will shew to you to day: for the Egyptians whom ye have seen to day, ye shall see them again no more forever."(Exodus 14:13)*

There are many types of fear according to psychology—phobophobia - the fear of fear; xenophobia - the fear of the unknown; metathesiophobia - the fear of change; atychiphobia - the fear of failure; aphenphosmphobia - the fear of intimacy; monophobia - the fear of being alone and thanatophobia - the fear of death. If you are experiencing any of these manifestations of fear you might be thinking there's no way out but what Moses said to the Israelites at the Red Sea, God says to you: "fear not, stand still and see the salvation of the Lord!" Though weeping may endure for the night, the psalmist said, but joy comes in the morning.

> *"Be strong and of a good courage, fear not, nor be afraid of them: for the Lord thy God, he it is that doth go with thee; he will not fail thee, nor forsake thee." (Deuteronomy 31:6)*

WORDS TO PONDER ON...

"The spirit of fear..."

> *"For God hath not given us the spirit of fear; but of power, and of love, and of a sound mind." (2 Timothy 1:7)*

Fear is a spirit—the spirit of Sanballat, Tobiah, and Geshem. It transcends what you can deal with psychologically; it requires spiritual warfare. To deal with fear, you need the Spirit of Power to pull down stronghold; the Spirit of Love because love never fails; and the Spirit of Sound Mind to apply godly wisdom to the situation at hand. The devil is cheap to deal with if you will just apply this divine prescription as highlighted in God's Word.

ASSIGNMENT

1. Do you easily give in to fear?
2. What are you afraid of?
3. What are you doing about it?
4. Have you reached out to someone for help?

Day 47

TACTIC #5: PROPAGANDA AS A TOOL OF MANIPULATION

"Then sent Sanballat his servant unto me in like manner the fifth time with an open letter in his hand; Wherein was written, It is reported among the heathen, and Gashmu saith it, that thou and the Jews think to rebel: for which cause thou buildest the wall, that thou mayest be their king, according to these words." (Nehemiah 6:5-6)

Nehemiah was confronted the fifth time with an open letter with surprising accusations. It was written and reported that Nehemiah and his men were about to rebel against the king that helped him with bearing the cost of rebuilding the wall. It was also said that he was planning to overthrow the king or take over that territory from the king. By any standard, these are serious allegations! But the good news is that they are false and like Nehemiah said, they were all fabricated.

This is another tactic of these wicked spirits to stop the work and the same tactic is still finding expression in our society today. It has been able to stop many from building or rebuilding their lives and it is called propaganda.

What is propaganda? Propaganda is a willful, prejudicial manipulation of information to inflict harm to the intended target. There are fifty different types of propaganda or different types of ways the enemy uses this to stop us from advancing our cause in life. One of the most common forms of propaganda the enemy uses is 'name calling'. For example, when someone decides to do better with his or her life and chooses to stop going out with a certain group of people, the first thing you might hear from these people usually comes in the form of a question: "Do you think that you are now better than us?" Or such a person might even be given a name all of a sudden, a name like 'Mr or Mrs Big Shot', or 'Obedient Boy/Girl' etc. That's propaganda and it seeks to get you to stop building or rebuilding your life in line with the word of God.

Another common form of propaganda is disinformation, which is the act of creating a false account or record by altering or removing the truth in order to mount up an opposition against the victim and appeal to his or her fear. This is usually done by people who know what gets you upset or afraid, so they play on your weakness. The enemy has used this type of propaganda to get people to do what they thought they would never do; it is the worst form of manipulation.

Let us look at this even in the life and ministry of Jesus. After Jesus resurrected, the watchmen came into the city and told the elders what actually happened, but instead of allowing the truth to prevail, they fabricated a lie that His disciples came at night and stole His body away.

> *"Now when they were going, behold, some of the watch came into the city, and shewed unto the chief priests all the things that were done.*

And when they were assembled with the elders, and had taken counsel, they gave large money unto the soldiers, Saying, Say ye, His disciples came by night, and stole him away while we slept. And if this come to the governor's ears, we will persuade him, and secure you. So they took the money, and did as they were taught: and this saying is commonly reported among the Jews until this day." (Matthew 28:11-15)

The problem with propaganda is that if it is not confronted it can cause a lot of damage. In the case of Jesus's resurrection, many Jews up till this present day would never believe that Jesus resurrected and they are still awaiting their own Messiah. If it happened to Jesus, it will happen to you. He was called many names, so get ready to fight the enemy's agenda.

WORDS TO PONDER ON...

"Greater is He..."

"Ye are of God, little children, and have overcome them: because greater is he that is in you, than he that is in the world." (1 John 4:4)

The One on the inside of you is greater than any lie anyone can tell against you. If you are not sure about anything, this scripture wants you know that you are of God, and that is great news knowing full well that you belong to God and have overcome the tactics of the enemy. You are larger than life when Jesus resides in you.

ASSIGNMENT

1. What does propaganda mean to you?
2. Have you seen this tactic working against you?
3. How can you stop this type of attack on you?
4. Are you sure the greater One is in you?

Day 48

TACTIC #6: FALSE PROPHECY AND DISTRACTION

"And, lo, I perceived that God had not sent him; but that he pronounced this prophecy against me: for Tobiah and Sanballat had hired him." (Nehemiah 6:12)

Nehemiah 6:1 opens up with a phrase of good news. *"Now it came to pass, when Sanballat, and Tobiah, and Geshem, and the rest of our enemies, heard that I had builded the wall, and there was no breach left therein…"* This is going to become your testimony soonest as you remain dedicated and committed to your plan of building or rebuilding so that there will be no more breach in your life.

Distraction is one of the last attacks of the enemy on our lives. The enemy may use any of the aforementioned combination of tactics to attack us, but when all else fails, the enemy will try to do anything to get us distracted. Nehemiah was invited to one of the villages in the plain of Ono so as to get him off his plan of completing the wall. He was invited four times—because the devil is more persistent than any of us. When the enemy attempts to distract us and he's not being successful, then he brings forth his last line of attack towards us: False prophecy!

Interestingly, some believers are addicted to prophecies—we could as well call them "the prophecy chasers". The devil who knows of this affinity then uses it against them. He knows you will believe in God and His word, so he attempts distraction by the use of false prophecy.

Nehemiah was deceived into meeting a man invited into the house of God within the temple, who gave a false prophecy to him about an impending attack against him. Thank God for the spirit of discernment! Nehemiah said "I perceived that God had not sent him, but he pronounced this prophecy against me: for Tobiah and Sanballat had hired him." This is very important. We need to be careful of those who call themselves Christians but who are rather wolves in sheep's clothing. As a matter of fact, your church or fellowship might become the best place for distractions to come under the disguise of prophecy or 'a word from God'. Please beware of anything that does not line up with the Word of God or any strange word of prophecy.

The story of the young and the old prophets readily comes to mind here. In 1 Kings 13, the Lord tells this young prophet to go and pronounce a judgment at a certain place and he is warned of God not to eat anything in the place. He comes in and carries out the instruction and leaves, but an older prophet comes to him on his way back and tells him that the Lord has spoken otherwise; he goes with the older prophet and eats and judgment falls swiftly on him as he is killed by a lion on his way home.

> *"For it was said to me by the word of the Lord, Thou shalt eat no bread nor drink water there, nor turn again to go by the way that thou*

> *camest. He said unto him, I am a prophet also as thou art; and an angel spake unto me by the word of the Lord, saying, Bring him back with thee into thine house, that he may eat bread and drink water. But he lied unto him. So he went back with him, and did eat bread in his house, and drank water. And it came to pass, as they sat at the table, that the word of the Lord came unto the prophet that brought him back:" (1 Kings 13:17-20)*

If God has not spoken to you directly, please be careful who you believe and as a fundamental rule, whatever you chose to believe must agree with the written Word of God; if it is not, you must not obey the instructions.

Other kinds of distractions are the cares of the world, the deceitfulness of riches, and the lusts of other things which can come in and choke the Word of God in our life—and anything that chokes the Word in our life is highly lethal!

> *"And the cares of this world, and the deceitfulness of riches, and the lusts of other things entering in, choke the word, and it becometh unfruitful." (Mark 4:19)*

WORDS TO PONDER ON...

"Attend upon the Lord without distraction..."

> *"And this I speak for your own profit; not that I may cast a snare upon you, but for that which is comely, and that ye may attend upon the Lord without distraction." (1 Corinthians 7:35)*

This Pauline advice is for our own good and not to dictate to us how we should live our lives. When we serve God without allowing distractions, the enemy will find it difficult to get the best of us.

ASSIGNMENT

1. What do you consider as a distraction?
2. Do you study your Bible regularly?
3. Do you understand what prophecy is?
4. Do you know how to detect a false prophecy?

Day 49

UNDER A BETTER COVENANT

"And hath raised us up together, and made us sit together in heavenly places in Christ Jesus:" (Ephesians 2:6)

Nehemiah was a strong leader. He commanded his troop to engage and fight the vicious spirits that confronted them and they defeated them all. He did all of these under the Old Testament, but we have a better covenant with better promises. Most importantly, we are filled with the Holy Spirit who knows all things—what a privilege! We are a chosen generation, a royal priesthood, a holy nation and peculiar people who have obtained mercy (1 Peter 2:9-10)

It is of utmost importance that you are born again because it is very difficult to fight these battles outside of God's covenant. As Prophet Jeremiah says, "It is of the Lord's mercies that we are not consumed, because his compassions fail not." (Lamentations 3:22). Moreover, Ephesians 1:19-22 tells us about the exceeding greatness of God's power towards us who believe:

"And what is the exceeding greatness of his power to us-ward who believe, according to the working of his mighty power, Which he wrought in Christ, when he raised him from the dead, and set him at his own right hand in the heavenly places, Far above all principality, and power, and might, and dominion, and every name that is named, not only in this world, but also in that which is to come: And hath put all things under his feet, and gave him to be the head over all things to the church."

What this means is that, if you have not made Christ your Savior and Lord, this kind of power is not available to you. Besides, the passage further reveals to us that we are seated with Christ far above principalities, powers, might and dominion, and every name (which includes all these spirits we have discussed) that is named, not only in this world, but also in that which is to come. What a glorious way to fight our enemies! The Scripture also says that if God is for us, who can be against us? (Romans 8:31).

Nehemiah had to fight with spears, swords and bows, but what weapons do we have? They are listed in Ephesians 6:13-17;

"Wherefore take unto you the whole armour of God, that ye may be able to withstand in the evil day, and having done all, to stand. Stand therefore, having your loins girt about with truth, and having on the breastplate of righteousness; And your feet shod with the preparation of the gospel of peace; Above all, taking the shield of faith, wherewith ye shall be able to quench all the fiery darts of the wicked. And take the helmet of salvation, and the sword of the Spirit, which is the word of God."

Firstly, we are clothed with the full armor of God (emphasis on 'full') by which we are able to withstand all the assaults of the devil in the evil day. Our weapons include girding our loins with the truth, putting on the breastplate of God's righteousness, shodding our feet with the preparation of the gospel of peace, and above all taking the shield of faith, wherewith we can stop all the fiery arrows of the devil. We are also to put on the helmet of salvation that gives us total access to God's blessings and, finally, the sword of the Spirit, which is the Word of God. It is evident that every enemy must bow to the Word of God, because the Word is the final authority and end of all arguments.

WORDS TO PONDER ON...

"He gave gifts unto men..."

> *"Wherefore he saith, When he ascended up on high, he led captivity captive, and gave gifts unto men." (Ephesians 4:8)*

The good news is that this scripture is very easy to believe. Why? It is evident that Jesus has already ascended up on high. If that is true, then the second part of the verse must also be true. It says that He led captivity captive—thereby narrowing down our enemy to just one: the devil. And if that's true, then the third part must also be true, which says that He gave gifts unto men. Every gift that you will need to achieve your goals has already been given to you and all you have to do is to activate them. Likewise, every material you need to build or rebuild your life has been given by the virtue of your position. Lay hold on them!

ASSIGNMENT

1. Are you born again?
2. Are you filled with the Holy Spirit?
3. Do you know your rightful position in Christ?
4. Have you discovered the gifts deposited in you?

Day 50

KINGDOM STEWARDSHIP

"But seek ye first the kingdom of God, and his righteousness; and all these things shall be added unto you." (Matthew 6:33)

Nehemiah was a man with a great heart for God. We discussed at the beginning how the condition of our heart is important for us to achieve our goals. Nehemiah did all that he did for the Kingdom's sake; there were no other motives. The condition of the people and the wall drove him to even risk his own life by appearing before the king moody. He did so much for the Kingdom that God promoted him from being a cupbearer to becoming the governor. Jesus tells us in Matthew 6:33 that we should "seek first the kingdom of God and His righteousness; and all these things shall be added" unto us. If God could do it in the Old Testament with Nehemiah, how much more will He do it under the better covenant and better promises of this dispensation?

When Kingdom stewardship becomes our lifestyle, then everything that others are dying to get will be added to us freely—and that includes everything we have already discussed in this book. How do I seek first the kingdom of God? I am sure that's the question you will like a straightforward and honest answer to, and I will do my best to explain it.

What was Jesus's mission on earth? His mission is revealed in Matthew 16:18-19 where He says "

> *And I say also unto thee, That thou art Peter, and upon this rock I will build my church; and the gates of hell shall not prevail against it. And I will give unto thee the keys of the kingdom of heaven: and whatsoever thou shalt bind on earth shall be bound in heaven: and whatsoever thou shalt loose on earth shall be loosed in heaven."*

Hence, we can as well say that seeking the Kingdom of God first means building the kingdom with Jesus. Apostle Paul reveals to us that God has chosen us co-workers with Him, thereby qualifying us to do all that is within our power by His to labor with Him in the vineyard.

> *"For we are labourers together with God: ye are God's husbandry, ye are God's building." (1 Corinthians 3:9)*

Every time you engage in Kingdom stewardship, you are helping Jesus build what the gates of hell cannot stop, and since you are also one of God's building projects, the gates of hell cannot prevail against you as you have practically become unstoppable by your enemies.

In case you are wondering how you can contribute to building God's Kingdom, we will consider five ways of doing this in the sections below. These include: praying for Kingdom advancement, evangelism, volunteering at church, providing for the poor, the widows and the fatherless, and giving tithes and offerings.

PRAYING FOR KINGDOM ADVANCEMENT

Most of the time (if not all the time), we become consumed with our needs that we spend all our prayer time asking God to meet our needs. My friend, while it definitely is not wrong to pray for ourselves, the most rewarding prayer you can ever pray is a prayer for the advancement of God's Kingdom. Apostle Paul tells us that

> *"I exhort therefore, that, first of all, supplications, prayers, intercessions, and giving of thanks, be made for all men; For kings, and for all that are in authority; that we may lead a quiet and peaceable life in all godliness and honesty." (1 Timothy 2:1-2)*

When we pray for all men, it will result in many more people coming into the Kingdom, and that is building the Kingdom with Jesus.

EVANGELISM

This is the most rewarding thing anybody can do—turning many unto the way of righteousness. The Bible says that he that wins a soul is wise (Proverbs 11:30). Evangelism is the heartbeat of God; if you want to build the kingdom with Jesus, you need to engage in evangelism and you will see your life improving effortlessly.

> *"And they that be wise shall shine as the brightness of the firmament; and they that turn many to righteousness as the stars for ever and ever." (Daniel 12:3)*

VOLUNTEERING AT YOUR LOCAL HOUSE OF WORSHIP

Jesus chose twelve disciples for His earthly ministry. He was able to replicate Himself in them, such that, when He left, the disciples took over the world and turned it upside down. The only way to bear a meaningful fruit that will abide is to engage in volunteering. There are many areas you could be of help—ask the leaders in your church and you will be surprised at how much you will be able to do. Volunteering is building the Kingdom with Jesus; your fruits are the gifts that you will need to build your own life.

> *"I am the vine, ye are the branches: He that abideth in me, and I in him, the same bringeth forth much fruit: for without me ye can do nothing." (John 15:5)*

PROVIDING FOR THE POOR, WIDOWS AND THE FATHERLESS

God does not owe any man, but when it comes to taking care of the poor, God has made Himself a debtor. The writer of Proverbs describes the act of giving to the poor as lending to the Lord (Proverbs 19:17)—and you can be assured that He will pay back. Matthew 25 amplifies this principle when Jesus says that He will separate the sheep and the goat, the sheep to the right side and the goat to the left side. As the passage goes on to tell us, the left side is hell which has been reserved for those who refuse to help the poor. There is no ambiguity whatsoever about this in the passage.

> *"For I was an hungred, and ye gave me meat: I was thirsty, and ye gave*

me drink: I was a stranger, and ye took me in: Naked, and ye clothed me: I was sick, and ye visited me: I was in prison, and ye came unto me. Then shall the righteous answer him, saying, Lord, when saw we thee an hungred, and fed thee? or thirsty, and gave thee drink? When saw we thee a stranger, and took thee in? or naked, and clothed thee? Or when saw we thee sick, or in prison, and came unto thee? And the King shall answer and say unto them, Verily I say unto you, Inasmuch as ye have done it unto one of the least of these my brethren, ye have done it unto me." (Matthew 25:35-40)

GIVING TITHES AND OFFERING

The Bible tells us to give and it shall be given back unto us good measure, pressed down and running over (Luke 6:38). Why would anyone not want to give? This promise is too sweet to be ignored! When you give, you are making provision for God's vision. When we give, honor is bestowed to God, and when we honor Him with our substance, our barn will be filled with plenty.

"Honour the Lord with thy substance, and with the firstfruits of all thine increase: So shall thy barns be filled with plenty, and thy presses shall burst out with new wine." (Proverbs 3:9-10)

WORDS TO PONDER ON...

"All My springs are in thee..."

"And of Zion it shall be said, This and that man was born in her: and the highest himself shall establish her. The Lord shall count, when he writeth up the people, that this man was born there. Selah. As well the singers as the players on instruments shall be there: all my springs are in thee." (Psalms 87:5-7)

Everything you need to make it—every material that will be required to build your life—is in Zion. If you are born into Zion then all the springs of your life are domiciled in Zion.

ASSIGNMENT

1. What is your prayer life like?
2. Do you go out for evangelism?
3. Are you a volunteer at your church?
4. Do you support the poor?
5. Are you a giver?

Day 51

PRAISE AND WORSHIP AS A WEAPON

"Let everything that hath breath praise the Lord. Praise ye the Lord." (Psalms 150:6)

Nehemiah praised God every moment he had the opportunity. He said many times that God should remember him for good (See Nehemiah 5:19, for example). But have you ever wondered—what could make God think about a man? When you praise and worship God, He comes down! The Bible tells us that God inhabits the praises of His people. Every time Nehemiah was delivered from the evil plans of Sanballat and his crew, he offered praise.

Praise and worship have tremendous power to deliver from a very strong opposition. There are a few good examples in the Bible, amongst which is the classic story of King Jehoshaphat. Three enemies came against this king—the children of Ammon, and Moab and Mount Seir—pretty much like Sanballat, Tobiah and Geshem. We are also faced with these types of enemies from time to time, and like Jehoshaphat, it is very normal to be overwhelmed and not know what to do; sometimes we might even feel very defenseless. All we need to do is to keep our eyes on the Lord and worship Him. Jehoshaphat was able to defeat these enemies by appointing singers unto the Lord whose responsibility was to praise the beauty of His holiness, and the Lord reacted swiftly. He set a trap for the enemies and they were smitten.

> *"And Jehoshaphat bowed his head with his face to the ground: and all Judah and the inhabitants of Jerusalem fell before the Lord, worshipping the Lord. And when he had consulted with the people, he appointed singers unto the Lord, and that should praise the beauty of holiness, as they went out before the army, and to say, Praise the Lord; for his mercy endureth for ever.*
>
> *And when they began to sing and to praise, the Lord set ambushments against the children of Ammon, Moab, and mount Seir, which were come against Judah; and they were smitten." (2 Chronicles 20: 18, 21-22)*

Another good example is the story of how the walls of Jericho came crashing down after the Israelites made a joyful noise to the Lord. What brought the wall down? Following God's simple instructions to go around the wall seven days and for the priests to blow the trumpets and the people to shout with a great shout.

> *"And it came to pass on the seventh day, that they rose early about the dawning of the day, and compassed the city after the same manner seven times: only on that day they compassed the city seven times. And it came to pass at the seventh time, when the priests blew with the trumpets, Joshua said unto the people, Shout; for the Lord hath given you the city. So the people shouted when the priests blew with the trumpets: and it came to pass, when the people heard the sound of the trumpet, and the people shouted with a great shout, that the wall fell*

down flat, so that the people went up into the city, every man straight before him, and they took the city." (Joshua 6:15-16, 20)

When you are confronted with the kinds of enemies that Nehemiah and the Israelites faced, all you need to do is to shout with a great shout! Habakkuk 3:17 tells us that even if we are yet to see any sign of victory, we are to continue praising the Lord Who then makes our feet like the deer's as He leads us to scale new heights and make advancement in life.

"Although the fig tree shall not blossom, neither shall fruit be in the vines; the labour of the olive shall fail, and the fields shall yield no meat; the flock shall be cut off from the fold, and there shall be no herd in the stalls: Yet I will rejoice in the Lord, I will joy in the God of my salvation. The Lord God is my strength, and he will make my feet like hinds' feet, and he will make me to walk upon mine high places..." (Habakkuk 3:17-19)

Joel 1:12 further says, "The vine is dried up, and the fig tree languisheth; the pomegranate tree, the palm tree also, and the apple tree, even all the trees of the field, are withered: because joy is withered away from the sons of men."

Without joy (which comes from praise and worship), our lives will dry up; joy is the lubricant that keeps our souls going against all the resistance the devil may bring our way. The Bible says let everything that has breath praise the Lord. If God gave us the breath of life with no conditions attached, then our praising Him should not have anything to do with whether He has done anything for us or not. If you want to build or rebuild your life, engage the weapon of praise and worship.

WORDS TO PONDER ON...

"O thou that inhabitest the praises of Israel"

"But thou art holy, O thou that inhabitest the praises of Israel." (Psalms 22:3)

God comes down when our praises go up. The only thing God cannot give Himself is praise—that's why He has twenty-four elders saying "Holy, Holy, Holy" all day long. Praise and worship are the most formidable weapons against any enemy. When God is praised, every knee must bow. If you are not happy with your situation, get your praise on and heaven will meet the earth and your story will change.

ASSIGNMENT

1. How often do you praise God?
2. Do you listen to worship music?
3. Are you the kind of person that always gets to church after the praise and worship session?
4. Have you tried praise and worship as a weapon in the past?

Day 52

THE MONTH OF ELUL

"So the wall was finished in the twenty and fifth day of the month Elul, in fifty and two days. And it came to pass, that when all our enemies heard thereof, and all the heathen that were about us saw these things, they were much cast down in their own eyes: for they perceived that this work was wrought of our God." (Nehemiah 6:15-16)

Nehemiah was successful in finishing the wall, against all odds—in a record time of fifty-two days. He refused to be distracted and bullied off the wall, and it came to pass that his enemies heard that the wall was completed. The Bible records that at the end of the day, his enemies lost their self-confidence. There are four lessons that we need to learn from this story; let's unpack them, beginning with the fact that the wall was completed in the month of Elul.

What is the month of Elul? In Jewish tradition, the month of Elul is a time of repentance—a time to search one's heart and draw close to God.

1. Deliverance from Sin

The first lesson is that God delivered the children of Israel from sin. Nehemiah confessed the sins of the people before he committed to rebuilding the wall and the wall was completed in the month Elul—which is the time of repentance. The lesson is that whether in trouble or triumph, our heart must be right with God.

2. Dare to Dream

The second lesson is that Nehemiah dared to dream. He had nothing but the news that the wall of Jerusalem had broken down. When he had the dream to rebuild, the provision miraculously showed up and every support needed from his brethren was also supplied by the good hand of the Lord.

3. Diligence: A Must

The third lesson is that the force of diligence must be at work in anyone who wants to build successfully. Nehemiah was a diligent man, and I believe that was the reason why he was the cupbearer; he was able to stand before the king. His diligence in the past with the king gave him the opportunity to ask for what he would need for the wall.

4. Determination and Dedication

The fourth lesson is that without determination and dedication we shall always be victims of circumstances. Nehemiah faced severe opposition—his life was threatened many times and lies were told against him—but through it all, he instructed his men to hold their weapons in one hand while building with the other. They were so committed that they only took off their clothes to have a shower; what a life of commitment, determination and dedication!

PROMOTED TO A GOVERNOR

Nehemiah was promoted from being a cupbearer to becoming the governor of the land of Judah. From a cupbearer to a governor? That could be only God. He engaged the problem of his people with a right heart—he was not looking for any personal gain, but was sincere. When these qualities are found together in one man, such is a candidate for promotion. Whenever you decide to build or rebuild your life with a pure motive, you have just signed your certificate of promotion. As you build or rebuild your life may the Almighty God elevate you.

> *"Moreover from the time that I was appointed to be their governor in the land of Judah, from the twentieth year even unto the two and thirtieth year of Artaxerxes the king, that is, twelve years, I and my brethren have not eaten the bread of the governor." (Nehemiah 5:14)*

WORDS TO PONDER ON...

"Promotion comes not from the east..."

> *"For promotion cometh neither from the east, nor from the west, nor from the south. But God is the judge: he putteth down one, and setteth up another." (Psalms 75:6-7)*

The thought to live a life of abundance comes from God. Anytime we accept responsibility for the happenings of our life, we move a step closer to promotion, which only comes from God. If God be for us who can be against us? God has settled your case because He's the righteous judge and He has decided that it is your turn to be enthroned. May it be it unto you according to His thoughts.

ASSIGNMENT

What have you learnt from this book?

May God richly bless you as you accept the personal responsibilities for the happenings of your life. You have delegated it long enough. Enough is enough!

ABOUT THE AUTHOR

Dr. Olalekan Joseph Olowe is a physical therapist by trade and a pastor by calling. Together with his wife, Omolade, they are the Presiding Servants over Kingdom Dominion Ministry International (KDMI) with a ministry base at El Paso, Texas from where they reach out globally.

A graduate of Rocky Mountain University of Health Professionals with a transitional Doctorate in Physical Therapy, Joseph is blessed with a physical therapy practice in El Paso, Texas.

He's a prolific writer and the author of I Am Three Dimensional, Living Free: The Power of Self-Control amongst other books. He's happily married to Omolade and they are blessed with three children.

KINGDOM DOMINION MINISTRY INTERNATIONAL
(KDMI)

To partner with us or to be part of Kingdom Dominion Ministry International (KDMI), please call or write us

1800-561-9170 or +1 915-478-8807

P. O Box 10499
El Paso, TX 79995

info@hisdominion.org I www.hisdominion.org